Kirsten Tibballs is a world-renowned pastry chef best known for everything chocolate. She is the star of *The Chocolate Queen*, which airs globally in over 40 countries and is now in its fourth season on SBS, and is a regular on *MasterChef* Australia as well as director of the Savour School, an online cooking school with a huge international following, as well as a bricks-and-mortar retail hub in Australia for chocolate and patisserie. Kirsten was the president of the jury for taste at the World Chocolate Masters in Paris, judge at the Patisserie Grand Prix in Japan and the World Chocolate Masters National selections in London. She is the global ambassador for Callebaut.

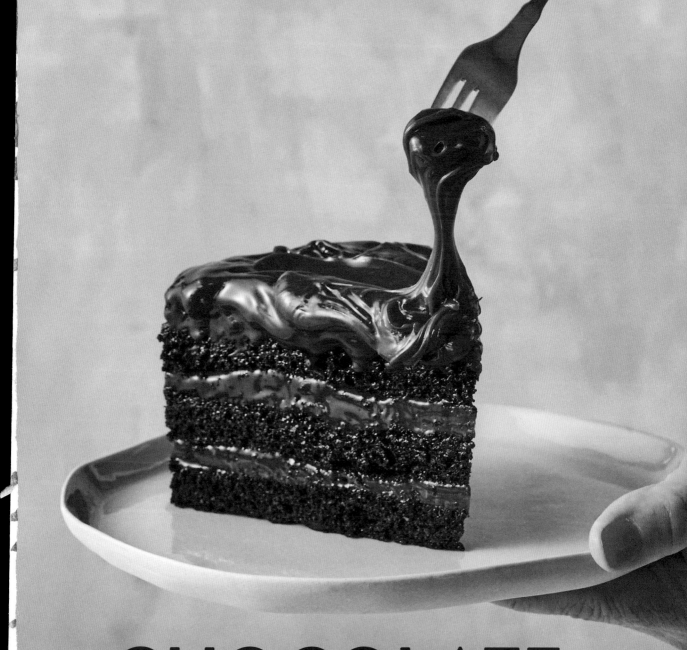

CHOCOLATE
ALL DAY

CHOCOLATE ALL DAY

Kirsten Tibballs

murdoch books

Sydney | London

For my son, Charlie

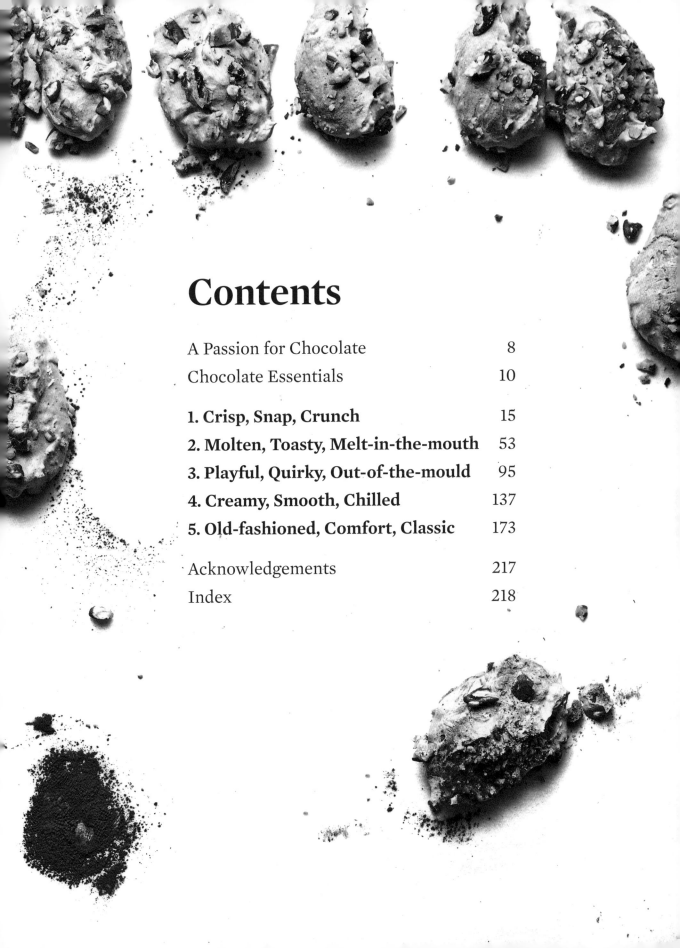

Contents

A Passion for Chocolate

I t's no secret that I have a passion for chocolate. In fact, a lifelong love affair might be a more accurate description! I love the joy it brings, the infinite wonders it can create and, of course, the incomparable taste. Chocolate is the ultimate ingredient, and I'm a firm believer that there's never a wrong time to enjoy it. *Chocolate All Day* is testament to this, and I hope within its pages you find the inspiration to explore, create and indulge whenever the mood strikes.

The foundations for this chocolate anthology were laid when I was just 12 years old.

While others were interested in science or sport or boys, I was enamoured with the kitchen. Cooking and feeding other people was my outlet, a by-product of an eating disorder that I struggled with in those early years. Before I'd turned 13, I had started taking orders, making a dozen birthday cakes every weekend. School fell away, and baking became my world.

At 15, when I had developed a healthier relationship with food, I began a patisserie apprenticeship.

I never looked back.

Thirty-five years later, I still love nothing more than sharing my passion for creating food and bringing people joy through my cooking. It's what motivated me to launch Savour, a first-of-its-kind chocolate and patisserie school, which helps cooks of all kinds create the incredible and unleash their amazing.

It's taken me around the world, from President of the Jury for Taste for the World Chocolate Masters, to the battleground of *MasterChef* challenges, including a history-making finale, and has set the stage for my very own TV Show, *The Chocolate Queen*.

It's motivated me to juggle running a business while raising a family and navigating a successful career – a journey made possible only with persistence and plenty of smiles, and one that I hope empowers the next generation of women.

And it's why I've spent hours, days and even weeks honing these recipes, and poured a lifetime of knowledge into each and every one. All to ensure that when you re-create them at home, you'll be rewarded with a truly wonderful chocolate treat.

None of the early mornings, late nights or perfected recipes would be possible without the unwavering support of my family. My husband, Michael, and my son, Charlie, are my part-time taste-testers and my full-time cheer squad, and I dedicate this book to them. And to the many, many other people who have supported my culinary adventures and helped turn this chocolate dream into a reality, I thank you in the only way I know how ... with 224 pages of molten, chilled, gooey, classic, sinful and spectacular chocolate goodness.

Kirsten Tibballs

Chocolate Essentials

I work with Callebaut brand chocolate and I use it in all the recipes in this book. If you can't get Callebaut, try to work with another good-quality chocolate, which can be referred to as couverture. I use chocolate in the form of buttons. You can use a block of chocolate, but you will need to chop it. To determine the quality, take a look at the ingredients. You want to ensure that the chocolate is made with cocoa butter and not vegetable fat. Chocolate made with vegetable fat is often referred to as compound chocolate. In compound chocolate the cocoa butter is replaced with a modified vegetable fat that has a higher melting point than cocoa butter, and both our palates and bodies find it difficult to process. Using compound chocolate will give you an inferior eating experience.

HOW AND WHY WE TEMPER CHOCOLATE

Chocolate only needs to be tempered if it is used as a coating or garnish. I have given instructions throughout the book in the relevant recipes on how to temper. I use the simple microwave method. However, if you don't have a microwave you can temper chocolate on the stovetop. (Refer to our Savour School YouTube channel, where you will find technique videos.) The reason why we temper chocolate is to avoid fat bloom. This is caused when the chocolate is melted without tempering. When the chocolate sets, some of the cocoa butter sets in larger particles, which can cause white dots or streaks throughout the chocolate. If your chocolate sets and it has fat bloom, it can be re-tempered as per my original tempering instructions, as long as nothing other than colour has been added to it.

HANDLING AND WORKING WITH CHOCOLATE

A small slab of stone is a great investment for working with chocolate. It will give you a flat surface that will pull the heat away from the chocolate. When working with chocolate, your room temperature should be no more than 24°C (75°F). You will sometimes need to use the fridge for setting chocolate. As a guide, a thin layer of chocolate shouldn't need more than 5 minutes in the fridge, and a thicker piece of chocolate up to 20 minutes. If you store chocolate in the fridge for longer periods of time, when you bring it to room temperature you will get condensation on the surface. The condensation will dissolve the sugar in the chocolate and it will set in larger particles, which you can see as well as feel on the palate.

HOW TO STORE CHOCOLATE

Chocolate should be well sealed in opaque
packaging at all times as it absorbs moisture
from the atmosphere very quickly, especially
in humid climates. If the chocolate has
absorbed moisture, its texture will be
noticeably thicker when melted. Use fresh
chocolate for finishing and garnishing.
If chocolate is exposed to light in clear
packaging, it will fade slightly in colour.

A NOTE ON EGGS

The recipes use 58 g (2 oz) eggs with the
shells (50 g/1¾ oz without). The 'whole egg'
weight refers to just the egg yolk and white
without the shell. If the weight needed is
more or less than a whole egg, lightly beat
the egg before weighing it to reach the
required quantity.

CHAPTER 1

Crisp, Snap, Crunch

Snap, Crackle & Choc Slice with Peanuts & Marshmallow

255 g (9 oz) white marshmallows
½ teaspoon vanilla bean paste
20 g (¾ oz) unsalted butter
70 g (2½ oz) puffed rice
30 g (1 oz) desiccated coconut
40 g (1½ oz) glacé cherries,
   chopped
30 g (1 oz) roasted
   peanuts, chopped
400 g (14 oz) good-quality
   milk chocolate chips
icing (confectioners') sugar,
   for dusting

This slice is loaded with the good stuff. A classic crispy puffed rice and coconut crackle spiked with glacé cherries, peanuts, marshmallows and last, but never least, plenty of chocolate! Satisfy your tastebuds by replacing the coconut, cherries and nuts with any other roasted nuts or dried fruit you desire. Just think of the possibilities.

Grease a 27.5 x 17.5 cm (11 x 6¾ inch) slice (slab) tin and line it with baking paper.

Place the marshmallows, vanilla and butter in a saucepan over very low heat and stir continuously until melted and combined.

Remove from the heat and add the puffed rice, coconut, cherries and peanuts, then mix with a spatula to combine.

In a microwave-safe plastic bowl, partially melt the milk chocolate in the microwave on high until you have 50% solids and 50% liquid, then add it to the marshmallow mixture in the pan and stir to combine.

Immediately transfer the mixture to the prepared tin and gently spread it out to the corners, being careful not to compact it.

Place the slice in the fridge for 15–20 minutes.

Remove the slice from the fridge and cut it into approximately 4 cm (1½ inch) squares.

Dust with icing sugar before serving.

To keep the slice crunchy, store in an airtight container for up to 2 weeks at room temperature below 25°C (77°F).

NEXT LEVEL
> Take the slice to a decadent new level by drizzling it with the ganache from my caramel slice recipe (see page 190).

White Chocolate Dacquoise with Cranberry & Pistachio

PISTACHIO & WHITE CHOCOLATE DACQUOISE

150 g (5½ oz) egg whites, at room temperature

pinch of cream of tartar

75 g (2½ oz) caster (superfine) sugar

70 g (2½ oz) pure icing (confectioners') sugar

50 g (1¾ oz) plain (all-purpose) flour

95 g (3¼ oz) ground pistachios

70 g (2½ oz) good-quality white chocolate

45 g (1½ oz) dried cranberries

90 g (3¼ oz) pistachios, chopped

TO FINISH

100–200 g (3½–7 oz) block good-quality white chocolate (the bigger the block, the bigger the curls)

20 g (¾ oz) dried cranberries

a few chopped pistachios

15 g (½ oz) pure icing (confectioners') sugar

Looking for your next lifelong romance? Try this nutty, meringue-style cake with a magic medley of white chocolate, pistachios and sweet cranberries. A vegetable peeler and a block of white chocolate are all you need to top this off in style. You can replace the pistachios, chocolate and cranberries with any other nuts or dried fruit.

For the pistachio and white chocolate dacquoise, preheat the oven to 170°C (325°F) fan-forced.

Grease and line a 21 x 11 cm (8¼ x 4¼ inch) loaf (bar) tin.

In a stand mixer with a whisk attachment, whisk the egg whites and cream of tartar, starting on a slow speed and gradually increasing it until you reach medium to firm peaks.

With the machine running, gradually add the caster sugar. Continue to whisk for 1 minute to allow the sugar to dissolve.

In a separate bowl, sift the icing sugar and flour, then add the ground pistachios.

Remove the bowl with the meringue from the mixer, then add the flour mixture and gently fold it through.

Add the chocolate, cranberries and approximately three-quarters of the chopped pistachios and fold them through.

Spoon the mixture into the prepared tin and gently level the surface with the back of a spoon. Sprinkle the remaining chopped pistachios on top.

Bake for 35 minutes.

Leave to cool in the tin for 15 minutes, then remove from the tin and leave to cool completely on a wire rack at room temperature.

You will always achieve bigger chocolate curls with slightly softened chocolate. Using a microwave is the best way to soften it. You can't place the chocolate on the base of the microwave as it will get too soft. I find I achieve best results by placing the chocolate in a microwave-safe plastic bowl. Test the chocolate consistency by pressing firmly with a vegetable peeler, starting

Continued overleaf >

FOR BEST RESULTS

> Make sure your egg whites are at room temperature before you start whisking. This will ensure you achieve better volume.

> Use older egg whites as they always whip up better than fresh egg whites.

on the corner of the chocolate and running down the length of the block. The thicker the block, the easier the curls are to make. If you are only getting small shavings, place the chocolate in the microwave on high for 10 seconds at a time, then continue testing until you are achieving bigger curls.

To finish, arrange the chocolate curls, dried cranberries and pistachios on top of the dacquoise, then dust with icing sugar.

This is best eaten at room temperature and stored in an airtight container in the fridge for 4 days. Bring it back to room temperature before eating. It can also be wrapped and stored in the freezer for up to 4 weeks before decorating.

If you only have buttons, you can make your own block of white chocolate by tempering the chocolate and then setting it in a bowl lined with plastic wrap. Place the chocolate in the base of the bowl and immediately place it in the fridge for 20 minutes before unmoulding and removing the plastic wrap.

Chocolate Pecan Meringue Bombs

220 g (7¾ oz) pecan nuts,
  roughly chopped
90 g (3¼ oz) egg whites,
  at room temperature
pinch of cream of tartar
250 g (9 oz) pure icing
  (confectioners') sugar, sifted
30 g (1 oz) Dutch-process cocoa
  powder, plus extra for dusting

FIX IT

> If the meringues become too soft at any stage, place them back in the oven at 110°C (225°F) for 20 minutes.

NEXT LEVEL

> I love to replace the pecans with the same weight of chopped almonds. You can also add a small amount – about 30 g (1 oz) – of finely chopped mixed peel for a fruity flavour.

> These meringues can be formed into any shape before baking. Try creating a wreath shape for the festive season – it may need an additional 10 minutes of baking.

Pecan and chocolate are a match made in flavour-combo heaven, and here they meet in chewy, nutty perfection. Whether you make them in neat rounds or free-form dollops, you're guaranteed a gorgeous result. Each bite will leave you craving more. Don't say I didn't warn you!

Preheat the oven to 150°C (300°F) fan-forced. Line a baking tray with baking paper.

Spread the pecans over the baking tray and bake for 12 minutes or until lightly roasted. Remove the pecans from the oven and reduce the oven to 110°C (225°F) fan-forced.

In the bowl of a stand mixer with a whisk attachment, whisk the egg whites with the cream of tartar – start whisking on a slower speed and gradually increase the speed until you achieve firm peaks. Reduce the mixer speed to low and gradually add the icing sugar. Continue to whisk for a further minute. Add the cocoa powder and whisk until just combined.

Remove the bowl from the mixer, add 180 g (6½ oz) of the pecans and gently fold them through.

Line two large baking trays with baking paper – use a small amount of the meringue under each corner to secure the paper. Use a lightly oiled teaspoon to place a generous scoop of the meringue on one of the trays, creating an oval about 4–5 cm (1½–2 inches) long. Repeat with the remaining meringue, leaving about 2 cm (¾ inch) between each meringue oval.

Sprinkle the remaining pecans over the meringues.

Bake for approximately 1½ hours, until the tops are shiny and feel firm.

Remove the trays from the oven and leave to cool at room temperature. Lightly dust with cocoa powder before serving.

Store the meringues in an airtight container at room temperature for up to 4 weeks.

Chocolate-coated Candied Popcorn

1 tablespoon coconut oil
  or vegetable oil
50 g (1¾ oz) plain popcorn kernels
150 g (5½ oz) caster (superfine)
  sugar
1 teaspoon sea salt
300 g (10½ oz) good-quality
  milk chocolate

What lies beneath the melt-in-the-mouth chocolate exterior is pure bliss in the form of caramelised popcorn. A little bit sweet, a little bit salty, and totally delicious. Every bite, with its spectacular ensemble of textures, will leave you giddy with excitement and reaching for another handful.

In a medium saucepan, heat the coconut oil over medium heat until hot and beginning to smoke slightly.

Add the popcorn kernels and immediately sit a sieve on top to seal the top of the saucepan.

As the kernels begin to pop, reduce the heat to low and shake the saucepan occasionally.

As the popping subsides, add the sugar to the sieve and shake the saucepan until the sugar has sifted through.

Continue to shake the pan until the sugar has caramelised – this will take a couple of minutes.

Remove the pan from the heat and stir the popcorn to ensure it is completely coated in caramel. Transfer to a sheet of baking paper and quickly separate the popcorn using a spatula.

Sprinkle the salt over the popcorn, then leave to cool completely at room temperature.

Temper the chocolate by placing it in a microwave-safe plastic bowl and heating it in the microwave on high in 30-second increments, stirring in between. Once you have 50% solids and 50% liquid, stir vigorously until the solids have completely melted. If you have some resistant buttons, you can gently heat the chocolate with a hair dryer while stirring to melt them.

Place the cooled popcorn in a bowl. Pour the tempered chocolate over the popcorn and stir to coat.

Create clusters by spooning tablespoons of the chocolate popcorn onto a sheet of baking paper. Leave to set at room temperature.

Store in an airtight container for up to 6 weeks below 25°C (77°F).

FOR BEST RESULTS

> Before coating in chocolate, seal the popcorn in airtight packaging and store it in the freezer. Bring it back to room temperature before opening.

> Test a couple of pieces of popcorn in the chocolate to make sure it sets before coating the full amount.

FIX IT

> If the chocolate begins to thicken or set while you are trying to coat the popcorn, reheat it with a hair dryer while stirring vigorously.

NEXT LEVEL

> Once the popcorn has been coated and the chocolate has set, brush with lustre powder or petal dust. This is also great if there are any blemishes on the chocolate.

Crunchy Chocolate & Peanut Butter Bark

200 g (7 oz) good-quality
  milk chocolate
35 g (1¼ oz) smooth
  peanut butter
20 g (¾ oz) roasted salted peanuts,
  roughly chopped

Three simple ingredients are all it takes to make magic, in this case in the form of decadent chocolate and peanut shards. Shamelessly sweet and salty, this easy-to-make bark is the perfect sneaky treat. There's no doubt about it, the creamy combination of peanut butter and chocolate, with the wondrous crunch of roasted peanuts, will satisfy you on the deepest of levels.

Temper the chocolate by placing it in a microwave-safe plastic bowl and heating it in the microwave on high in 30-second increments, stirring in between. Once you have 50% solids and 50% liquid, stir vigorously until the solids have completely melted. If you have some resistant buttons, you can gently heat the chocolate with a hair dryer while stirring to melt them.

Spread half of the tempered chocolate over a sheet of baking paper to a thickness of approximately 5–7 mm (¼ inch). Leave to set at room temperature.

As soon as it sets, spread a thin layer of peanut butter over the chocolate.

If required, reheat the remaining chocolate with a hair dryer, then spread it over the top of the peanut butter with a palette knife.

Before the chocolate sets, sprinkle with the roasted peanuts.

Place in the fridge for 5 minutes to set.

Once the bark has completely set, break into pieces and enjoy.

The bark can be stored for up to 4 weeks in an airtight container at room temperature below 25°C (77°F).

FIX IT

> If the chocolate doesn't set, place it in the freezer and serve directly from the freezer.

NEXT LEVEL

> This recipe is amazing made with dark chocolate.

> You can replace the peanut butter with any other nut paste.

Jewelled Pistachio & Cherry Chocolate Snowflakes

20 g (¾ oz) desiccated coconut

150 g (5½ oz) good-quality milk chocolate

20 g (¾ oz) glacé cherries, finely chopped

20 g (¾ oz) pistachios, finely chopped

Delicate, decorative and with a sprinkling of pistachios and glacé cherries for added flavour, colour and fun. A sensory delight of melt-in-your-mouth chocolate with a satisfying crunch. If you're not vibing with pistachios, cherries and coconut, switch them with your favourite medley of nuts and dried or glacé fruit for your ultimate snowflake. These are just as delicious made with white or dark chocolate.

Preheat the oven to 160°C (315°F). Line a baking tray with baking paper.

Spread the coconut evenly over the baking tray and bake for 5–6 minutes. Remove from the oven halfway through baking to stir, which will ensure you achieve an even colour. Once golden brown, remove from the oven and leave to cool completely at room temperature.

You will need to cut 15 individual snowflake templates out of baking paper, approximately 9 cm (3½ inches) in diameter (see photo overleaf). To do this, start with a 10 cm (4 inch) square of paper. Fold it in half, then in half again to create a smaller square. Fold the two folded edges together to create a triangle. Fold the two folded edges together again to create a narrower triangle. Trim off the excess paper at the open end of the triangle so that all layers of the triangle are the same size, then trim the open edge in a zigzag shape. Along the long folded edge of the triangle, cut a half-oval shape – the longer it is, the bigger the oval will be on the snowflake. Open out the paper. Repeat to make 15 templates.

Temper the chocolate by placing it in a microwave-safe plastic bowl and heating it in the microwave on high in 30-second increments, stirring in between. Once you have 50% solids and 50% liquid, stir vigorously until the solids have completely melted. If you have some resistant buttons, gently heat them with a hair dryer while stirring to melt them.

Place the templates on a flat surface and spread the chocolate over them using a small palette knife or a brush. Make sure the chocolate is thick enough and as even as possible to help prevent cracking.

Continued overleaf >

FOR BEST RESULTS

> Once the chocolate has set on your snowflakes, cover the tray with another sheet of baking paper and place a second baking tray on top, which will help to prevent the chocolate from curling as it contracts. Leave the tray on top for at least an hour.

> Don't make the chocolate too thin (it should be at least 2 mm/1/16 inch thick) or the snowflakes will break as you remove the baking paper.

NEXT LEVEL

> Remember that in nature no two snowflakes are the same, so experiment with different-shaped templates.

> Why stop at snowflakes? Create hearts for that special valentine.

Working quickly, sprinkle the coconut, cherries and pistachios over the melted chocolate.

Before the chocolate sets, use a small knife to help lift each snowflake, with its template, and place on a tray lined with baking paper. Scrape the excess chocolate into a bowl, so it can be used again.

Once set, carefully remove the baking paper template from each snowflake.

The snowflakes can be made up to 3 months in advance and stored in an airtight container at room temperature below 25°C (77°F).

Caramelised Mille Feuille Stack with Chocolate Custard

CARAMELISED FILO PASTRY

8 filo pastry sheets

100 g (3½ oz) unsalted butter, melted

60 g (2¼ oz) soft brown sugar

CHOCOLATE CUSTARD

500 ml (17 fl oz) full-cream milk

1 teaspoon vanilla bean paste

20 g (¾ oz) custard powder or cornflour (cornstarch)

100 g (3½ oz) caster (superfine) sugar

200 g (7 oz) egg yolks

310 g (11 oz) good-quality dark chocolate (57% cocoa)

140 g (5 oz) unsalted butter, cubed

TO FINISH

pure icing (confectioners') sugar, for dusting

Probably the most impressive thing a sandwich press has ever turned out, this clever chocolate custard mille feuille transforms store-bought filo into a simple yet sensational pastry affair. Caramelised pastry and luscious chocolate custard unite as an unapologetically sinful and satisfying treat. With elements that can be prepared in advance, this is the perfect show-stopping dessert for your next dinner party.

To make the caramelised filo pastry, brush a sheet of filo pastry with some of the melted butter and sprinkle an eighth of the brown sugar evenly over the surface.

Layer the remaining seven sheets of pastry on top, brushing with the butter and sprinkling with the sugar each time.

Cut the filo stack in half lengthways, then cut each half into six even rectangles, to create 12 rectangles in total.

Heat a sandwich press.

Cook the pastry rectangles in the sandwich press, two at a time, for approximately 30 seconds, until golden.

Remove the pastry from the sandwich press, place between two sheets of baking paper and place a baking tray or weight on top to help prevent the pastry from curling.

Repeat with the remaining pastry rectangles, cleaning the sandwich press between batches.

(The pastry can also be baked in a 190°C/375°F oven, between two sheets of baking paper with a baking tray on top and another underneath, until golden brown.)

Leave to cool completely at room temperature.

Store the pastry flat in an airtight container until ready to assemble. (The pastry can be made 1 day in advance.)

For the chocolate custard, heat the milk and vanilla in a saucepan over medium heat and bring to the boil.

Meanwhile, combine the custard powder and sugar in a bowl.

Continued overleaf >

FOR BEST RESULTS

> Don't step away from
  the sandwich press as the
  pastry will cook in seconds.

Add the yolks and whisk by hand.

While whisking, pour the hot milk over the mixture.

Transfer the mixture back to the saucepan and bring to the boil while continuously whisking.

Put the chocolate in a bowl.

Pour the custard over the chocolate and whisk until the chocolate is completely melted and incorporated.

Add the butter, a piece at a time, and whisk until incorporated and smooth.

Cover with plastic wrap touching the surface of the custard, then place in the fridge for a minimum of 4 hours. (The custard can be made up to 3 days in advance.)

To assemble, transfer the chilled custard into a piping bag fitted with a 1.6 cm (⅝ inch) plain tip.

Pipe individual dots of custard onto four of the caramelised pastry rectangles – five or six rows of three works well. Alternatively, you can just spread the custard over the pastry.

Top each with a second pastry rectangle and pipe another layer of custard on top, then place a final pastry rectangle on top.

Lastly, dust with icing sugar.

To ensure the pastry stays crunchy, assemble just before serving.

Peanut Cookie Cups with Chocolate Caramel Filling

PEANUT COOKIE CUPS

85 g (3 oz) unsalted butter
65 g (2¼ oz) soft brown sugar
65 g (2¼ oz) caster (superfine)
  sugar
95 g (3¼ oz) crunchy peanut butter
30 g (1 oz) whole egg
125 g (4½ oz) plain (all-purpose)
  flour, plus extra for dusting
pinch of baking powder
pinch of sea salt
75 g (2½ oz) good-quality milk
  chocolate, chopped

CARAMEL FILLING

250 ml (9 fl oz) thickened
  (whipping) cream
1 teaspoon vanilla bean paste
pinch of sea salt
185 g (6½ oz) caster (superfine)
  sugar
65 g (2¼ oz) liquid glucose
35 ml (1¼ fl oz) water
150 g (5½ oz) unsalted butter
25 g (1 oz) honey
½ teaspoon bicarbonate of
  soda (baking soda)
75 g (2½ oz) good-quality
  milk chocolate

Just when you thought a chocolate and peanut flavour combo couldn't get any better. Here, a biscuity peanut butter base acts as a little bowl for lush honeyed caramel, with chocolate whisked through in the final step because, well … chocolate. Believe me, you will fall in love with these wickedly irresistible caramel cups.

To make the peanut cookie cups, preheat the oven to 170°C (325°F) fan-forced. Grease a 12-hole muffin tin.

Using a stand mixer with a paddle attachment, beat the butter and sugars on medium speed until well combined and completely smooth.

Add the peanut butter followed by the egg and mix to combine.

Add the flour, baking powder and salt, then mix until almost completely incorporated.

Lastly, add the chopped milk chocolate and mix until the ingredients just come together as a dough.

On a lightly floured work surface, divide the dough into 12 even portions.

Place the pieces of dough into the holes in the tin, pressing them into the base and sides to form a cup.

Line each cup with scrunched then flattened baking paper, and fill with uncooked rice. Bake for 8 minutes. (This is called blind baking.)

Remove the paper and rice and bake for a further 10 minutes.

Leave to cool slightly. When the cookie cups are firm enough to handle but still warm, remove from the tin and leave to cool completely at room temperature on a wire rack.

Clean and dry the muffin tin.

When the cookie cups have cooled completely, return them to the clean tin.

Continued overleaf >

NEXT LEVEL

> This recipe can also make one spectacular large tart. Press the cookie dough into a fluted flan (tart) tin, then follow the recipe. Serve slices with fresh cream or ice cream.

> The peanut cookie cup mixture can be used to make beautiful cookies.

For the caramel filling, heat the cream, vanilla and salt in a saucepan over medium heat until almost boiling.

Heat the sugar, glucose and water in a large saucepan over medium heat until the temperature reaches 145°C (293°F).

Reduce the heat to low, immediately add the butter and honey and whisk by hand to incorporate.

One-third at a time, pour the hot cream mixture over the caramel and whisk to combine.

Carefully add the bicarbonate of soda, then increase the heat and bring to 118°C (244°F) while whisking continuously.

Once the caramel reaches temperature, remove from the heat and immediately add the chocolate. Whisk until the chocolate is completely melted and incorporated.

Pour the caramel into the prepared peanut cookie cups and leave to set at room temperature for 1 hour.

Store in an airtight container at room temperature for up to 4 weeks.

Chocolate Coconuts

6 milk chocolate Easter eggs with a
   smooth finish and approximately
   7 cm (2¾ inches) long
85 g (3 oz) pure icing
   (confectioners') sugar, sifted
75 g (2½ oz) desiccated coconut
65 ml (2¼ fl oz) sweetened
   condensed milk
½ teaspoon lemon juice

Imagine luscious, smooth milk chocolate colliding with rough yet sweet coconut to create an enthrallingly seductive flavour and mouthfeel. This super-easy coconutty treat is a fabulous way to transform left-over Easter egg chocolate. With a simple brushing technique and a sweet, textured centre to crack into, these ordinary eggs become magnificent mini coconuts. Prepare yourself for this blissfully sweet tropical treat.

Warm a baking tray in the oven at 50°C (120°F).

Place a knife in a jug of warm water for a few minutes. Carefully cut the chocolate eggs in half with the hot knife, keeping both halves intact – use a paper towel to hold the eggs and prevent them from melting in your hands.

Place a clean tea towel on your work surface, then remove the hot baking tray from the oven and place it on the towel.

Working with two egg halves at a time, carefully place the cut sides down on the warm tray to melt the edges slightly and create more of a coconut shape. Do not apply pressure as the eggs can break easily.

Place the eggs in the fridge for 2–3 minutes to solidify slightly, then remove and set aside at room temperature.

Put the icing sugar, desiccated coconut, condensed milk and lemon juice in a bowl and mix to combine. Spoon a small amount of the mixture into each coconut half and, holding the chocolate shell in paper towel, gently spread it out with the back of a teaspoon to create a coconut layer.

Place the chocolate coconuts in the fridge for 2–3 minutes.

With a clean, firm-bristled toothbrush or wire brush, gently brush the outside of each chocolate shell using a downward motion until it resembles the husk of a coconut. Give an extra brush over the seam to ensure the shell has the same texture all over.

The chocolate coconuts can be made up to 1 week in advance. They may need to be rebrushed before serving.

Store in an airtight container for up to 6 weeks at room temperature below 25°C (77°F).

FOR BEST RESULTS

> If you have warm hands, freeze the chocolate shells for 5–10 minutes before brushing.

> Use a brush with firm bristles. The firmer the bristles, the more definition you will achieve on the chocolate shell.

NEXT LEVEL

> For the ultimate dessert, use these cheeky chocolate coconuts as a bowl for ice cream or mousse.

Glazed Chocolate Mousse Cake with a Crunch

CRUNCH LAYER

95 g (3¼ oz) good-quality milk
  chocolate (33% cocoa)
160 g (5½ oz) crunchy
  peanut butter
30 g (1 oz) puffed rice,
  slightly crushed
20 g (¾ oz) candied orange fillets
  (optional), finely chopped

CHOCOLATE MOUSSE

vegetable oil spray, for greasing
pure icing (confectioners') sugar,
  for dusting
370 ml (12½ fl oz) thickened
  (whipping) cream
340 g (11¾ oz) good-quality
  dark chocolate (54% cocoa)
65 ml (2¼ fl oz) water
65 g (2¼ oz) caster (superfine)
  sugar
65 g (2¼ oz) liquid glucose

CHOCOLATE GLAZE

8 gelatine sheets of any variety
bowl of chilled water, for soaking
335 ml (11½ fl oz) thickened
  (whipping) cream
100 ml (3½ fl oz) water
505 g (1 lb 2 oz) caster (superfine)
  sugar
170 g (6 oz) Dutch-process
  cocoa powder, sifted
100 g (3½ oz) liquid glucose

TO FINISH

30 g (1 oz) Dutch-process
  cocoa powder

With its galaxy-like surface, there's something other-worldly about this decadent dark chocolate mousse cake. A sneaky layer of peanut butter and puffed rice adds a crunch and that little something extra. Want to make a lasting impression? This shiny, sleek show stopper is the ultimate never-to-be-forgotten cake for your next event. Note that you need to start the cake the day before you serve it.

To make the crunch layer, line a 16 cm (6¼ inch) round cake ring with baking paper and place on a baking tray lined with baking paper.

Temper the chocolate by placing it in a microwave-safe plastic bowl and heating it in the microwave on high in 30-second increments, stirring in between. Once you have 50% solids and 50% liquid, stir vigorously until the solids have completely melted. If you have some resistant buttons, you can gently heat the chocolate with a hair dryer while stirring to melt them.

Add the peanut butter and mix to combine.

Add the puffed rice and candied orange, if using. Mix until they are completely coated in chocolate.

Spread the crunch layer into the prepared cake ring. Press down gently with the back of a spoon to level the mixture.

Place in the fridge.

For the chocolate mousse, prepare an 18 cm (7 inch) cake ring by greasing it with vegetable oil and dusting with icing sugar, then place it on a baking tray lined with baking paper.

Semi-whip the cream until it has some body but still collapses. Set aside in the fridge until required.

Partially melt the dark chocolate in the microwave in a microwave-safe plastic bowl until you have 50% solids and 50% liquid. Set aside.

Combine the water, caster sugar and glucose in a saucepan over medium heat and bring to the boil.

FOR BEST RESULTS

> Use a very fine sieve, such as a tea strainer, when sifting the cocoa powder over the glaze, as you don't want too much cocoa powder to come out at once.

> If the glaze is too thick, the cocoa powder won't crack and spread when it's sifted on top. You can thin out the glaze by adding a couple of drops of water at a time.

NEXT LEVEL

> Instead of adding the cocoa powder on top of the glaze, decorate the cake with the chocolate flower from my chocolate cheesecake tart recipe (page 169).

Once the sugar has completely dissolved, pour the syrup over the partially melted chocolate and whisk to combine. Leave the chocolate to cool to just above body temperature.

Mix a small amount of the semi-whipped cream through the chocolate mixture before adding the remaining cream and folding it through.

Remove the ring and baking paper from the prepared crunch layer and place it in the centre of the 18 cm (7 inch) cake ring.

Pour the chocolate mousse over the crunch layer. Use a palette knife to level the top. Place in the freezer overnight.

The next day, make the chocolate glaze. Soak the gelatine sheets in the bowl of chilled water.

Place the cream, water and sugar in a saucepan over medium heat and bring to the boil. Add the cocoa powder and liquid glucose and whisk to combine. Bring to the boil again before removing the pan from the heat and transferring to a jug or bowl.

Squeeze the excess water out of the gelatine before adding it to the glaze. Mix until smooth using a stick blender.

Cover the glaze with plastic wrap touching the surface and leave to cool to between 32 and 35°C (90 and 95°F).

Once the glaze has cooled, push the frozen cake up from the base to remove it from the ring.

Line a baking tray with sides with baking paper. Place an overturned bowl or cake tin on the tray. Sit the frozen cake on top of the bowl and pour the glaze over the cake. Immediately sift the cocoa powder over the surface of the cake.

Once the glaze stops dripping, use a sharp knife to trim the excess glaze from around the base of the cake.

Transfer the cake to a serving plate and place in the fridge for a minimum of 4 hours before serving.

The excess glaze can be stored in an airtight container in the freezer for up to 8 weeks. To reuse the glaze, reheat it in the microwave, adding a little water if the glaze is too thick.

You can store the unglazed cake in the fridge for up to 4 days or in the freezer for up to 8 weeks. Once glazed, the cake can be stored in the fridge for up to 3 days.

Pictured overleaf >

Pineapple White Chocolate Nougat with Almonds & Coconut

50 g (1¾ oz) pure icing
  (confectioners') sugar
50 g (1¾ oz) cornflour (cornstarch)
90 g (3¼ oz) egg whites,
  at room temperature
pinch of cream of tartar
440 g (15½ oz) caster (superfine)
  sugar
250 g (9 oz) honey
80 ml (2½ fl oz) pineapple juice
125 ml (4 fl oz) water
90 g (3¼ oz) liquid glucose
bowl of chilled water
150 g (5½ oz) good-quality
  white chocolate
220 g (7¾ oz) whole almonds,
  roasted and kept warm
100 g (3½ oz) desiccated coconut

A hit of pineapple juice and lashings of coconut put a tropical spin on this snowy white chocolate and roasted almond nougat. Just one bite of this seductively chewy treat will transport you to a sun-drenched paradise. This nougat makes a great gift if cut into bars and wrapped in cellophane. These need to be sealed as soon as they're cut so they don't absorb moisture from the atmosphere.

Grease and line a 23 cm (9 inch) square tin with baking paper.

In a bowl, combine the icing sugar and cornflour.

Sift a fine layer of the icing sugar and cornflour mixture into the prepared tin. Set the remaining mixture aside.

Place the egg whites, cream of tartar and 25 g (1 oz) of the caster sugar in a stand mixer with a whisk attachment.

In a saucepan, combine the honey and pineapple juice.

In a separate saucepan over medium heat, heat the water, the remaining caster sugar and the glucose to 110°C (230°F), then begin heating the honey and pineapple mixture over medium heat. Keep heating the sugar and glucose.

Once the honey mixture reaches 105°C (221°F), begin to whisk the egg whites on high speed.

When the honey mixture reaches 130°C (266°F), pour it over the egg whites while continuing to whisk.

Once the sugar and glucose mixture reaches 170°C (325°F), pour it over the egg whites while continuing to whisk.

Change the whisk to a paddle attachment and continue to mix. (To remove the mixture from the whisk, dip your clean fingers in the bowl of chilled water and run them along each wire.)

Test the consistency of the nougat by placing a small amount in the bowl of chilled water. The texture should be firm. If the mixture is too soft, apply some heat to the outside of the mixer bowl with a hair dryer to evaporate the excess moisture.

Continued overleaf >

NEXT LEVEL

> For some extra chocolatey goodness, use a toothpick to dip the nougat in tempered chocolate of your choice.

> Instead of pineapple, you could try your favourite juice flavour.

When you reach the correct consistency, add the white chocolate and mix to combine.

Mix in the warm almonds and coconut.

Pour the mixture into the prepared tin, then dust the top with some more of the icing sugar and cornflour mixture. Press the nougat to create a flat, even surface.

Leave to set at room temperature until cool.

Remove from the tin and use a serrated knife to cut the nougat into 3 cm (1¼ inch) squares (or leave in long strips), dusting with the icing sugar and cornflour mixture as you go to prevent the nougat from sticking.

Store in an airtight container at room temperature below 25°C (77°F) for up to 6 weeks.

Chocolate-dipped Coconut Bars

250 g (9 oz) pure icing
   (confectioners') sugar, sifted
225 g (8 oz) desiccated coconut
200 ml (7 fl oz) sweetened
   condensed milk
1½ teaspoons vanilla extract
1½ teaspoons lemon juice
250 g (9 oz) good-quality
   dark chocolate
20 g (¾ oz) shredded coconut,
   for sprinkling

A sweet coconut centre dunked in rich, decadent dark chocolate. This is the perfect treat if you catch yourself craving something indulgent, and makes an unforgettable offering when unexpected guests drop in. Be warned, though, as these simple yet stunning little bars are easy to devour and will disappear fast.

Line the base and sides of a slice (slab) tin – approximately 27.5 x 17.5 cm (11 x 6¾ inches) and 3.5 cm (1¼ inches) high – with baking paper.

In a bowl, combine the icing sugar and desiccated coconut.

Add the condensed milk, vanilla and lemon juice and mix to combine.

Press the mixture into the prepared tin and place in the fridge for a minimum of 2 hours.

Once the coconut slab is firm, cut it into 16 individual bars.

Temper the chocolate by placing it in a microwave-safe plastic bowl and heating it in the microwave on high in 30-second increments, stirring in between. Once you have 50% solids and 50% liquid, stir vigorously until the solids have completely melted. If you have some resistant buttons, you can gently heat the chocolate with a hair dryer while stirring until they melt.

Press a toothpick into the top of each bar, or balance the bar on a large fork, to dip it into the tempered chocolate. Gently tap the fork on the edge of the bowl to remove any excess chocolate, then transfer the coconut bars to a tray lined with baking paper.

Before the chocolate sets, finish by sprinkling the shredded coconut over half of the bar in a diagonal shape.

Leave the chocolate to set completely before serving.

Store in an airtight container for up to 6 weeks at room temperature below 25°C (77°F).

FIX IT

> If the chocolate is not tempered correctly and develops a few streaks, brush the outside of the bars with cocoa powder or dust with icing sugar for a sweeter finish.

CHAPTER 2

Molten, Toasty, Melt-in-the-mouth

Oozy Chocolate Sourdough Toastie

75 ml (2¼ fl oz) full-cream milk

120 ml (4 fl oz) sweetened
  condensed milk

100 g (3½ oz) whole eggs

pinch of sea salt

pinch of ground cinnamon

2 teaspoons unsalted butter

1 teaspoon grapeseed oil

8 slices day-old sourdough bread,
  crusts removed

2 bananas, thinly sliced lengthways

80 g (2¾ oz) good-quality milk
  chocolate chips

This is no ordinary toastie – more like a sinful chocolate snack. It's an amped-up version of French toast, layered with slivers of banana and dotted with melting chocolate chips, and is best devoured hot and fresh. The molten, magnificent mess that's created between two sweetened slices of bread is unbelievable. This is bound to be bookmarked as a favourite.

Put the milk, condensed milk, eggs, salt and cinnamon in a bowl and whisk to combine.

Transfer the mixture to a shallow dish.

Heat the butter and oil in a frying pan over medium heat.

Dip each slice of bread in the condensed milk mixture, then place in the frying pan and cook both sides until golden brown.

Remove from the heat.

Arrange the banana in an even layer over four of the bread slices, sprinkle with chocolate chips, then sandwich together with the remaining bread.

The toasties are best made fresh and served immediately.

FOR BEST RESULTS

> Don't use bread with large air pockets.

> Have all the elements ready to go before you start frying the bread.

NEXT LEVEL

> I love replacing the banana with fresh or sautéed pineapple.

Choc-chip Cookie Sandwiches with Orange Ganache

ORANGE GANACHE

195 ml (6¾ fl oz) thickened (whipping) cream
zest of 1 orange
½ teaspoon vanilla bean paste
430 g (15¼ oz) good-quality milk chocolate

COOKIES

100 g (3½ oz) raw sugar
165 g (5¾ oz) soft brown sugar
1 teaspoon sea salt
115 g (4 oz) unsalted butter, softened
50 g (1¾ oz) whole egg
1 teaspoon vanilla bean paste
155 g (5½ oz) plain (all-purpose) flour
½ teaspoon bicarbonate of soda (baking soda)
110 g (3¾ oz) good-quality milk chocolate, roughly chopped
110 g (3¾ oz) good-quality dark chocolate, roughly chopped
90 g (3¼ oz) cornflakes, crushed

Make way for your new obsession. I'm talking chewy cookies with a lusciously smooth, melt-in-the-mouth filling with hints of crunch. A little bit fancy, and a whole lot of fun, these choc-chip cornflake cookies get a flavour boost thanks to a swirl of orange-infused chocolate ganache. They are a tantalising eating experience and an instant crowd pleaser.

To make the orange ganache, heat the cream, orange zest and vanilla in a saucepan over medium heat and bring to the boil.

Place the milk chocolate in a bowl.

Once the cream is boiling, strain it over the chocolate. Whisk until the chocolate is completely melted and incorporated into the cream.

Cover with plastic wrap touching the surface of the ganache. Leave to cool at room temperature for 2–3 hours before transferring to a piping bag or snaplock bag.

For the cookies, preheat the oven to 170°C (325°F) fan-forced. Line a baking tray with baking paper.

Place the raw sugar, brown sugar, salt and butter in the bowl of a stand mixer with a paddle attachment and beat on medium speed until smooth.

Add the egg and vanilla and mix to combine.

Sift in the flour and bicarbonate of soda and mix until incorporated.

Remove the bowl from the mixer, add the chocolate and crushed cornflakes and stir them through.

Place the cookie dough in the fridge for 1 hour.

Roll teaspoonfuls of the dough into balls. Place them on the baking tray approximately 4 cm (1½ inches) apart and gently press down on them to flatten slightly.

Bake for 10 minutes or until golden brown.

Continued overleaf >

FOR BEST RESULTS

> If your room temperature is warm, place the ganache in the fridge to firm it up to piping consistency.

FIX IT

> If the ganache looks grainy after you add the cream to the chocolate, add a tiny bit more cream and continue whisking.

Remove from the oven and leave to cool at room temperature. Repeat with the remaining cookie dough.

To assemble, cut the tip off the prepared piping bag of orange-infused ganache.

Pipe the ganache onto every second cookie and sandwich them together with the plain cookies.

Store in an airtight container at room temperature for up to 2 weeks.

The cookie dough can be prepared in advance and stored in an airtight container in the fridge for up to 3 days. Allow the dough to come back to room temperature before baking.

Espresso Chocolate Truffles with Honey & Vanilla

260 ml (9¼ fl oz) thickened
(whipping) cream

20 g (¾ oz) roasted coffee beans,
crushed

1 teaspoon honey

1 teaspoon vanilla bean paste

pinch of sea salt

520 g (1 lb 2½ oz) good-quality
milk chocolate

150 g (5½ oz) Dutch-process
cocoa powder

FOR BEST RESULTS

> If you have hot hands,
cool them on a bag
of frozen peas before
rolling the truffles.

NEXT LEVEL

> The coffee can be replaced
with spices, such as
cinnamon, star anise
or vanilla.

> Instead of cocoa powder,
roll the truffles in crushed
roasted nuts.

**Surrender yourself to these simple and irresistible morsels –
the most indulgent way to get a coffee hit. Small in size but
big on flavour, these to-die-for truffles are laden with chocolate
and coffee goodness and mellowed with a touch of honey and
vanilla. They also make excellent gifts, if you can bring yourself
to part with them.**

Heat the cream in a saucepan over medium heat and bring
to the boil.

Remove from the heat and add the coffee beans. Place the lid
on the saucepan and leave to infuse for 10 minutes.

Strain the cream into another saucepan, then add the honey,
vanilla and salt and bring to the boil over medium heat.

In a microwave-safe plastic bowl, partially melt the chocolate
in the microwave on high in 30-second increments until you
have 50% solids and 50% liquid.

Pour the hot cream over the chocolate, then whisk until the
chocolate is completely melted and incorporated.

Cover with plastic wrap touching the surface of the ganache
and leave to set at room temperature for a minimum of 8 hours,
or overnight.

Roll teaspoons of the ganache into balls to make truffles.

Place the cocoa on a plate or in a shallow bowl, then roll the
truffles in the cocoa powder to coat.

Store in an airtight container at room temperature below 25°C
(77°F) for up to 1 week.

Chocolate Pain Perdu
with Rum & Raisin

PAIN PERDU

190 ml (6½ fl oz) full-cream milk

1 star anise

2 vanilla beans, split lengthways
   and seeds scraped

20 g (¾ oz) caster (superfine) sugar

40 g (1½ oz) egg yolks

90 g (3¼ oz) good-quality
   white chocolate

75 ml (2¼ fl oz) thickened
   (whipping) cream

1 good-quality long baguette
   (enough for 6–8 people)

pure icing (confectioners') sugar,
   for dusting

RUM & RAISIN
CHOCOLATE SPREAD

30 g (1 oz) raisins, roughly chopped

30 ml (1 fl oz) rum

20 ml (½ fl oz) thickened
   (whipping) cream

100 ml (3½ fl oz) sweetened
   condensed milk

10 g (¼ oz) salted butter

100 g (3½ oz) good-quality
   milk chocolate

This unassuming recipe is one of my absolute favourites in this book. A baguette twist on pain perdu (French toast), taken up a notch thanks to the very welcome addition of white chocolate. Smother it with a layer of silky rum and raisin chocolate spread and you're onto a winner. This is the perfect way to impress your guests at your next brunch.

To make the pain perdu, combine the milk, star anise and vanilla in a saucepan over medium heat and bring to the boil.

Meanwhile, whisk the sugar and egg yolks in a small bowl.

Place the white chocolate in a bowl.

Pour the hot milk mixture over the yolks while whisking, then transfer the mixture back to the saucepan. Reduce the heat to low and heat, stirring, until it reaches 80°C (176°F).

Immediately strain the custard over the white chocolate. Whisk until the chocolate is completely melted and incorporated. Add the cream and whisk to combine.

Preheat the oven to 250°C (500°F) fan-forced. Line a baking tray with baking paper.

Cut the baguette into 1 cm (½ inch) slices and dip them in the custard mixture, then place them on the baking tray.

Dust the surface of each baguette slice with a layer of icing sugar.

Bake for 6–7 minutes, until golden.

Leave to cool at room temperature.

For the rum and raisin chocolate spread, put the raisins in a small bowl, pour the rum over them, then cover the bowl with plastic wrap. Leave to sit for as long as possible.

Heat the cream in a saucepan over medium heat and bring to the boil.

Add the condensed milk and butter, then stir over low heat until completely combined and the butter has melted.

Place the chocolate in a bowl.

Continued overleaf >

FOR BEST RESULTS

> Pain perdu is the traditional name for this recipe and means 'lost bread', referring to older stale bread. The recipe won't be as good with fresh bread.

> Don't leave the bread slices in the oven for too long or the crusts will go too dark.

NEXT LEVEL

> For the ultimate decadent experience, serve the toast with crème brûlée, or top it with ice cream.

Pour the hot mixture over the chocolate and stir until the chocolate is completely melted and incorporated.

Add the soaked raisins and any excess rum, then mix to combine.

Cover with plastic wrap touching the surface of the spread and leave to set at room temperature for 2 hours before serving.

The pain perdu is best eaten the same day. The spread is best kept in a cool, dry place for up to 1 week – it will become too firm to spread if stored in the fridge.

Glossy Chocolate Brioche Buns

250 g (9 oz) baker's flour
25 g (1 oz) caster (superfine) sugar
5 g (⅛ oz) salt
12 g (½ oz) instant yeast
150 g (5½ oz) whole eggs,
  at room temperature
50 ml (1½ fl oz) water,
  at room temperature
pinch of ground cinnamon
pinch of ground nutmeg
125 g (4½ oz) unsalted butter,
  at room temperature, cubed
125 g (4½ oz) good-quality milk
  chocolate, roughly chopped
vegetable oil spray, for greasing

EGG WASH
50 g (1¾ oz) whole egg
1 teaspoon full-cream milk

Think light, soft, pillowy buns – a simple brioche dough bursting with chocolate bits and just the right amount of spice. Are you more of a brioche loaf lover? No problem. This recipe can be used to create the most fabulous loaf – simply increase the baking time. These glossy little buns are sensational served warm. You'll need to start them a day ahead as they need to prove overnight.

Place the flour, sugar, salt and yeast in the bowl of a stand mixer with a dough hook attachment and mix on medium speed for approximately 1 minute.

Place the eggs and water in a bowl and whisk to combine.

Stream the egg mixture into the flour mixture with the mixer on low–medium speed.

Add the cinnamon and nutmeg and mix to incorporate – ensure there are no dry ingredients remaining on the bottom of the bowl. Continue to mix on medium speed for 10 minutes.

With the mixer running, gradually add the butter cubes over 5 minutes. Once the butter has been incorporated, continue to mix for a further 15 minutes.

Lastly, add the chocolate and mix to incorporate.

Transfer the dough to a bowl lightly greased with vegetable oil spray and cover tightly with plastic wrap. Set aside to prove at room temperature for 30 minutes.

Place in the fridge overnight.

Lightly spray your work surface, scales and hands with vegetable oil spray, then divide the dough into 10 pieces and roll into balls.

Place the buns on a baking tray lined with baking paper, ensuring there is space between them to allow them room to spread out.

Cover loosely with plastic wrap and leave to sit at room temperature for 3½–4 hours.

Continued overleaf >

FOR BEST RESULTS

> It's best to leave the butter out at room temperature overnight.

> You can stop the process of the dough developing at any stage by freezing it.

NEXT LEVEL

> Add some dried fruit to the dough at the same time as you add the chocolate for some additional pops of flavour.

> Pipe a cross on top of the buns to convert these to hot cross buns.

Make an egg wash by whisking the egg and milk in a bowl to combine. Set aside.

Preheat the oven to 170°C (325°F) fan-forced.

Brush the surface of the buns with the prepared egg wash, then bake for 13 minutes, until golden brown.

Remove the buns from the oven and leave them to cool slightly before serving.

The buns are best eaten within 2–3 days of baking. Store them in an airtight container at room temperature.

Steamed Chocolate Puddings with Hot Fudge Sauce

CHOCOLATE PUDDINGS

2 x 50 g (1¾ oz) whole eggs

100 g (3½ oz) unsalted butter, softened

1 teaspoon vanilla extract

50 g (1¾ oz) caster (superfine) sugar

50 g (1¾ oz) soft brown sugar

105 g (3½ oz) self-raising flour, sifted

pinch of sea salt

100 g (3½ oz) good-quality dark chocolate

60 ml (2 fl oz) thickened (whipping) cream

150 g (5½ oz) good-quality milk chocolate chips

CHOCOLATE FUDGE SAUCE

150 g (5½ oz) good-quality milk chocolate

200 ml (7 fl oz) thickened (whipping) cream

30 ml (1 fl oz) golden syrup (light treacle)

TO FINISH

125 g (4½ oz) fresh raspberries

Who doesn't love a steamed, saucy choccy pudding? The decadent chocolate chips and hot, glossy fudge sauce are why I always come back to this fail-safe recipe. Warning: You may be overcome by the irresistible chocolatey scent of these luscious molten puddings. They are what sweet dreams are made of.

To make the chocolate puddings, preheat the oven to 140°C (275°F) fan-forced.

Place the eggs, in their shells, in a bowl of lukewarm water to warm them to body temperature.

In the bowl of a stand mixer with a paddle attachment, combine the butter, vanilla and caster and brown sugars, then beat on medium–high speed until light and fluffy.

Crack the warmed eggs into a separate bowl and lightly beat by hand to break them up. With the mixer running on medium speed, gradually add the egg to the butter mixture.

Remove the bowl from the mixer, add the flour and salt and gently fold them through.

Melt the dark chocolate in a microwave-safe plastic bowl in the microwave on high in 30-second increments, stirring in between, until completely melted.

Fold the melted chocolate and cream through the batter, followed by the milk chocolate chips.

Evenly divide the mixture among five 250 ml (9 fl oz) ovenproof bowls or ramekins.

Cover each bowl with a disc of greased baking paper and a piece of foil, then place the bowls in a large, deep-sided baking tin or baking dish. Pour boiling water into the tin until it reaches halfway up the bowls.

Carefully place the baking tin in the oven and bake for approximately 40 minutes, until the puddings have risen and are firm to the touch, and when a skewer inserted into the centre comes out clean.

Continued overleaf >

NEXT LEVEL

> These puddings look delightful when made in decorative ovenproof coffee cups.

For the chocolate fudge sauce, put the chocolate in a bowl.

Heat the cream and golden syrup in a small saucepan over medium heat until the mixture begins to boil.

Remove from the heat, pour the mixture over the chocolate and whisk to combine.

Transfer the sauce to a serving jug.

Top the puddings with a little of the chocolate sauce and serve with the raspberries. Serve with the left-over sauce in the jug on the table for people to help themselves.

The puddings are best enjoyed fresh out of the oven. However, you can make them the day before and store them in the fridge unbaked. Bake them fresh, and eat while hot.

The sauce can be made the day before. Cover with plastic wrap touching the surface and reheat before serving.

Chocolate, Cinnamon & Caramel Scrolls

DOUGH

240 ml (8 fl oz) full-cream milk

16 g (½ oz) instant yeast

70 g (2½ oz) caster (superfine)
   sugar

70 g (2½ oz) whole eggs,
   at room temperature

30 g (1 oz) egg yolk,
   at room temperature

80 g (2¾ oz) unsalted butter,
   melted

540 g (1 lb 3 oz) baker's flour,
   plus extra for dusting

¾ teaspoon salt

FILLING

60 g (2¼ oz) butter, softened

60 g (2¼ oz) soft brown sugar

pinch of ground cinnamon

120 g (4¼ oz) good-quality milk
   chocolate, roughly chopped

vegetable oil spray, for greasing

SUGAR SYRUP

100 g (3½ oz) caster (superfine)
   sugar

60 ml (2 fl oz) water

CHOCOLATE GLAZE

100 g (3½ oz) pure icing
   (confectioners') sugar

1 tablespoon water

½ teaspoon Dutch-process
   cocoa powder

pinch of ground cinnamon

It's time to get cosy with my scrumptious scrolls. The scent alone makes them worth making, but once that medley of cinnamon, caramel notes of brown sugar and milk chocolate hits your mouth, you'll understand why they're a staple at my place. You can even have them baked fresh for breakfast.

To make the dough, warm the milk in a saucepan over low heat to 40°C (104°F), then transfer to the bowl of a stand mixer with a dough hook attachment.

Sprinkle the yeast over the milk, then add the caster sugar, whole egg, egg yolk and melted butter. Mix on medium speed to combine.

Add the flour and salt and mix until the dough comes together, about 2 minutes.

Continue mixing on medium speed for 8 minutes, or knead by hand for the same length of time.

Once the dough forms a slightly sticky ball, remove from the mixer and place in a lightly oiled bowl. Cover the bowl with plastic wrap and a warm towel, then leave the dough to sit at room temperature for up to 1½ hours, until it doubles in size.

Place the dough on a lightly floured work surface and roll into a 35 x 30 cm (14 x 12 inch) rectangle.

To fill the scrolls, spread the softened butter evenly over the dough, leaving a 1.5 cm (⅝ inch) strip on the long edges of the rectangle.

Combine the brown sugar and cinnamon in a small bowl, then sprinkle it over the butter. Use the back of a spoon to spread it out evenly.

Sprinkle the chocolate on top of the sugar and cinnamon.

Starting from the nearest short edge, tightly roll up the dough, then adjust the roll to ensure the seam is underneath.

Use a sharp knife to cut the dough into 12 equal portions, approximately 2.5 cm (1 inch) wide.

Continued overleaf >

FIX IT

> If your dough doesn't rise, it's because the yeast is dead. This can happen for a few reasons – either the yeast is old or the milk was too hot.

NEXT LEVEL

> For freshly baked scrolls for breakfast, leave the scrolls in the fridge for 12–14 hours overnight to slowly rise. Bring them back to room temperature before baking.

Lightly spray a 32 x 22 cm (12¾ x 8½ inch) baking tin with vegetable oil spray.

Arrange the scrolls evenly in the tin, ensuring a cut side is facing up.

Cover with plastic wrap and a warm towel. Leave to sit at room temperature for 40–45 minutes.

Preheat the oven to 170°C (325°F) fan-forced.

Bake the scrolls for 20 minutes or until just golden brown.

Prepare the sugar syrup while the scrolls are baking. Heat the sugar and water in a small saucepan over medium heat and bring to the boil. Continue to boil for 1–2 minutes to create a syrup.

Brush the scrolls with the syrup immediately after removing them from the oven. Leave to cool slightly while preparing the chocolate glaze.

Mix all the glaze ingredients in a bowl to combine.

Drizzle the chocolate glaze over the slightly cooled scrolls.

The scrolls are best eaten the same day they are baked, but will keep for up to 2 days in an airtight container at room temperature. The scrolls can be prepared and frozen for up to 4 weeks at any stage before baking.

Golden Tartlets with Baked Hazelnut Cream & Caramel Chocolate

PASTRY

150 g (5½ oz) unsalted butter, cubed

100 g (3½ oz) soft brown sugar

30 g (1 oz) hazelnut meal

50 g (1¾ oz) whole egg

260 g (9¼ oz) plain (all-purpose) flour, plus extra for dusting

½ teaspoon salt

½ teaspoon baking powder

BAKED HAZELNUT CREAM

75 g (2½ oz) whole eggs

50 g (1¾ oz) caster (superfine) sugar

35 g (1¼ oz) hazelnut meal

25 g (1 oz) lightly roasted hazelnuts, roughly chopped

HAZELNUT CARAMEL

35 g (1¼ oz) good-quality gold caramel chocolate (or use milk chocolate)

35 g (1¼ oz) honey

120 ml (4 fl oz) thickened (whipping) cream

zest of 1 orange

1 teaspoon vanilla bean paste

35 g (1¼ oz) liquid glucose

½ teaspoon sea salt

95 g (3¼ oz) caster (superfine) sugar

70 g (2½ oz) roasted hazelnuts, roughly chopped

Gorgeously gooey and loaded with roasty, toasty hazelnuts, these golden gems are always a crowd-pleaser. The contrasting textures and a spot of orange zest make them unforgettable. The tarts are spectacular as individual tartlets, or as a single large tart. Either way, you will experience pure, indulgent enjoyment with every bite.

For the pastry, arrange 12 egg rings, approximately 7.5 cm (3 inches) in diameter and 1 cm (½ inch) high, on a baking tray lined with baking paper.

Place the butter in the bowl of a stand mixer with a paddle attachment and beat on medium speed until smooth.

Add the brown sugar, hazelnut meal and egg and mix until combined.

Add the flour, salt and baking powder and continue to mix until the ingredients come together as a dough. Once the dough forms, stop mixing to ensure you don't develop the gluten, which will make the pastry tough and chewy.

Press the dough into an even, flat square and wrap it in plastic wrap. Place in the fridge for approximately 30 minutes.

Preheat the oven to 170°C (325°F) fan-forced.

Lightly dust the work surface with flour and roll the dough out until it is approximately 3 mm (⅛ inch) thick. Cut 12 discs out of the dough using a 9.5 cm (3¾ inch) round cutter.

Transfer the pastry discs to the egg rings, press it into the base and sides and trim any overhang.

Line the pastry with scrunched then flattened baking paper, and fill with uncooked rice. Bake for 10 minutes. (This is called blind baking.)

Remove the rice and baking paper and set the pastry aside at room temperature until required.

For the baked hazelnut cream, preheat the oven to 165°C (320°F) fan-forced.

> Ensure the pastry is chilled before rolling it out. Only roll half the pastry at a time and keep the other half in the fridge.

> Don't waste the pastry offcuts from the first half of the dough; instead press them into the remaining dough before rolling.

> When making the caramel, only stir gently, as vigorous movement will recrystallise the sugar as it melts.

Place the eggs, caster sugar and hazelnut meal in a bowl and mix to combine.

Add the roughly chopped hazelnuts and fold them through.

Spoon the mixture into the prepared tart shells, until each shell is half full.

Bake for 10–12 minutes, until light golden brown.

For the hazelnut caramel, place the gold caramel chocolate in a bowl and set aside.

Combine the honey, cream, orange zest, vanilla, glucose and salt in a small saucepan over medium heat and bring to the boil.

Once boiled, strain the cream mixture through a sieve into a bowl. Set aside and keep warm.

Place the sugar in a wide-based saucepan over medium heat. Stir gently with a spatula until completely dissolved and caramelised before removing from the heat. If the sugar is caramelising quickly and you still have lumps of sugar, lower the temperature to allow the sugar to dissolve before the caramel burns.

Carefully add the warm cream mixture to the caramel and whisk to combine.

Return the saucepan to the stovetop and cook over low heat for 1 minute.

Pour the caramel over the chocolate and stir until the chocolate is completely melted and incorporated into the caramel.

Add the hazelnuts and mix to combine.

Remove the tarts from the rings and spread the caramel over the baked hazelnut cream in the tarts.

Store in an airtight container at room temperature for up to 4 days.

The caramel can be made a day in advance. Cover it with plastic wrap touching the surface and set aside at room temperature until required. To soften the caramel, simply microwave in short increments until it reaches a scoopable consistency.

Pictured overleaf >

Choc-chip & Swiss Meringue Doughnuts with Chocolate Sauce

CHOC-CHIP DOUGHNUTS

190 ml (6½ fl oz) full-cream milk

35 ml (1¼ fl oz) warm water, approximately 35°C (95°F)

7 g (¼ oz) instant yeast

60 g (2¼ oz) whole eggs, beaten

40 g (1½ oz) caster (superfine) sugar

¾ teaspoon salt

325 g (11½ oz) plain (all-purpose) flour, plus extra for dusting

35 g (1¼ oz) unsalted butter, softened

150 g (5½ oz) good-quality milk chocolate chips

vegetable oil, for deep-frying (approximately 3 litres/105 fl oz)

SWISS MERINGUE

150 g (5½ oz) caster (superfine) sugar

pinch of cream of tartar

75 g (2½ oz) egg whites, at room temperature

60 g (2¼ oz) good-quality dark chocolate

CHOCOLATE TOPPING

100 ml (3½ fl oz) thickened (whipping) cream

1 tablespoon liquid glucose

1 tablespoon coconut oil

175 g (6 oz) good-quality dark chocolate

These are no ordinary doughnuts. They are the type of doughnuts you dream about, with a light doughy centre and silky yet fudgy adornment. The wow factor is without a doubt the luscious chocolate marbled meringue topping. They might just be the ultimate sweet treat.

To make the doughnuts, gently heat the milk in a medium saucepan over low heat until just warm.

Pour the warm water into the bowl of a stand mixer with a paddle attachment and sprinkle the yeast on top. Let it stand for 5 minutes.

After 5 minutes, add the warm milk, egg, caster sugar, salt and half the flour, then mix on medium speed to combine.

Swap the paddle to a dough hook and mix for 1 minute before adding the remaining flour. Mix until the dough pulls away from the side of the bowl, 8–10 minutes.

Continue mixing on medium speed for 4 minutes to develop the gluten.

With the mixer running, gradually add the softened butter, a little at a time. Once all the butter has been added, continue to mix for a further 4 minutes. The dough will be quite soft.

Lastly, add the chocolate chips and mix them in.

Transfer the dough to a lightly oiled large bowl and cover with a damp tea towel. Leave to sit at room temperature for 1 hour.

Once doubled in size, knock the air out of the dough by punching it.

Place the dough on a lightly floured work surface and roll it out to 1 cm (½ inch) thick.

Cut with either a doughnut cutter or a 6 cm (2½ inch) round cutter for the outside, and a 2 cm (¾ inch) cutter for the hole. Place the doughnuts on individual 10 cm (4 inch) squares of baking paper.

Continued overleaf >

FOR BEST RESULTS

> Keep some of the doughnut centres and use them to test whether the oil is hot enough.

NEXT LEVEL

> The coconut oil in the chocolate topping gives a great flavour and incredible shine, but it can be replaced with cream.

Lightly dust the doughnuts with flour and cover with a clean, damp tea towel. Leave to rest at room temperature for a further 30 minutes.

Pour the vegetable oil into a deep-fryer or large heavy-based saucepan and heat the oil to 170°C (325°F).

Using metal tongs, carefully lower 1–3 doughnuts into the oil (depending on the size of your pan) and cook for approximately 1 minute on each side, until golden brown.

Carefully remove the doughnuts from the oil using tongs and place on a plate lined with paper towel to absorb the excess oil. Repeat with the remaining doughnuts.

Leave to cool at room temperature for 20 minutes.

For the Swiss meringue, place the sugar, cream of tartar and egg whites in a heatproof bowl that will sit stably on the top of a saucepan and whisk to combine.

Place the bowl over a saucepan of simmering water, making sure the bowl doesn't touch the water, and cook, while whisking, until the mixture reaches 60°C (140°F).

Transfer the mixture to the bowl of a stand mixer with a whisk attachment and whisk on medium speed until the meringue cools and forms firm peaks.

Meanwhile, heat the chocolate in a microwave-safe plastic bowl in the microwave on high in 30-second increments, stirring in between, until completely melted.

Add the melted chocolate to the meringue and continue to mix for a further minute.

Set aside at room temperature.

For the chocolate topping, heat the cream, glucose and coconut oil in a saucepan over medium heat and bring to the boil.

Place the dark chocolate in a bowl and pour the hot liquid over the top. Whisk until the chocolate is completely melted and incorporated.

Spread the Swiss meringue on top of the doughnuts.

Drizzle the chocolate topping over the meringue and marble it slightly using a teaspoon.

These doughnuts are best eaten the day they are made. Store them at room temperature until you are ready to serve.

Sticky Date Chocolate Puddings with Chocolate Caramel Drizzle

CHOCOLATE GANACHE CENTRE

75 g (2½ oz) good-quality dark
    chocolate
50 ml (1½ fl oz) thickened
    (whipping) cream

CARAMEL SAUCE

75 ml (2¼ fl oz) thickened
    (whipping) cream
¼ teaspoon sea salt
175 g (6 oz) caster (superfine) sugar
125 g (4½ oz) unsalted butter,
    cubed
50 g (1¾ oz) good-quality milk
    chocolate
75 g (2½ oz) liquid glucose

DATE PUDDINGS

vegetable oil spray, for greasing
95 g (3¼ oz) plain (all-purpose)
    flour, sifted, plus extra for dusting
140 g (5 oz) pitted dates, roughly
    chopped
½ teaspoon bicarbonate of soda
    (baking soda)
125 ml (4 fl oz) boiling water
40 g (1½ oz) unsalted butter,
    softened
20 g (¾ oz) soft brown sugar
55 g (2 oz) whole eggs, at room
    temperature
¾ teaspoon baking powder
30 g (1 oz) good-quality milk
    chocolate chips

What could make a hot, steamy, sticky date pudding more irresistible? Chocolate … obviously. These sensational date puddings drip with sticky, chocolate-spiked caramel sauce. Now for the surprise: dig your spoon in to reveal a lust-worthy chocolate ganache centre.

To make the ganache centre, heat the chocolate in a microwave-safe plastic bowl in the microwave on high in 30-second increments until 50% melted.

Heat the cream in a small saucepan over medium heat until bubbles just begin to appear. Take care not to let the cream boil as the quantity is very small and you do not want too much liquid to evaporate.

Pour the hot cream over the semi-melted chocolate and whisk until the chocolate is completely melted and incorporated into the cream. Leave to set at room temperature.

Spoon six equal portions of the ganache onto a baking tray lined with baking paper. Place in the freezer for a minimum of 4 hours to freeze completely.

For the caramel sauce, combine the cream and salt in a saucepan over medium heat and bring to the boil. Remove from the heat and set aside.

Place the sugar in a wide-based saucepan over medium heat. Stir gently with a spatula until completely dissolved and caramelised before removing from the heat. If the sugar is caramelising quickly and you still have lumps of sugar, lower the temperature to allow the sugar to dissolve before the caramel burns.

Carefully pour the warm cream over the caramel and whisk over low heat to combine.

Remove from the heat and add the butter, one piece at a time, while whisking by hand.

Put the chocolate in a bowl. Once the butter is completely incorporated, add the glucose and stir it in, then pour the mixture over the chocolate. Stir until completely melted and combined.

Continued overleaf >

FIX IT

> If the first pudding you unmould breaks, leave them for a little longer in the ramekins before unmoulding.

NEXT LEVEL

> If you love caramel sauce, double the recipe for some extra caramel goodness.

Cover with plastic wrap touching the surface of the caramel and set aside at room temperature.

For the date puddings, prepare six 100 ml (3½ fl oz) ramekins or ovenproof coffee cups by spraying them with oil, then dusting with a thin layer of flour.

Preheat the oven to 165°C (320°F).

Place the dates in a bowl and sprinkle with the bicarbonate of soda. Pour the boiling water on top and leave to stand at room temperature for 10 minutes before using a potato masher to break up the dates into a chunky paste.

In a stand mixer with a paddle attachment, beat the butter and brown sugar on medium speed until completely smooth.

Break the eggs into a bowl and place it in a warm water bath (a larger bowl of warm water) to warm slightly. Slowly add the eggs to the butter mixture and beat to combine.

Add the flour and baking powder and mix until incorporated.

Working quickly, add the date paste and chocolate chips and mix until well incorporated into the batter.

Divide half of the mixture evenly among the prepared ramekins or cups.

Place the prepared frozen ganache in the centre of each ramekin, then cover with the remaining batter.

Bake for 15–17 minutes, until the puddings are lightly golden on top and wobbly in the centre.

Leave to cool at room temperature for a few minutes before carefully removing the puddings from the ramekins by turning them upside down. (You don't have to unmould the puddings – you can serve them in their baking dishes.)

Place the puddings right-side up on a serving plate, top with caramel sauce and serve while hot.

You can make the puddings the day before and store them in the fridge, unbaked. Bake them fresh, and eat while hot. The sauce can be made the day before – cover with plastic wrap touching the surface until ready to serve.

The unbaked puddings can also be stored in the freezer before baking. Leave them to thaw at room temperature or in the fridge before baking.

Poached Pears with Ginger–Chocolate Ganache in White Chocolate Nests

GINGER–CHOCOLATE GANACHE

480 g (1 lb 1 oz) good-quality
  milk chocolate
240 ml (8 fl oz) thickened
  (whipping) cream
15 g (½ oz) liquid glucose
30 ml (1 fl oz) ginger juice
  (squeezed through a sieve
  from grated fresh ginger)
pinch of ground ginger
pinch of sea salt
70 g (2½ oz) unsalted butter, cubed

POACHED PEARS

6 pears, ripe but still firm
750 ml (26 fl oz) moscato wine,
  or other sweet dessert wine
400 g (14 oz) caster (superfine)
  sugar
400 ml (14 fl oz) water
1 cinnamon stick, broken in half
2 tablespoons honey
2 cm (¾ inch) piece fresh ginger,
  peeled and finely chopped
1 teaspoon vanilla bean paste

WHITE CHOCOLATE NESTS

200 g (7 oz) good-quality
  white chocolate

The flavours, the textures, the techniques ... I cannot prepare you for how enthralling this dessert is. Whole pears poached in moscato that's gently spiced with ginger, filled and coated in silky ganache, then placed in a nest of thinly piped white chocolate. If you're after 'wow', look no further.

To make the ginger–chocolate ganache, place the milk chocolate in a bowl.

In a saucepan over medium heat, combine the cream, glucose, ginger juice, ground ginger and salt, then bring to the boil.

Pour the hot mixture over the chocolate and whisk until the chocolate is completely melted and incorporated.

Keep whisking while adding the butter, one piece at a time, until smooth and shiny.

Cover with plastic wrap touching the surface of the ganache and set aside at room temperature for 5 hours to firm up.

For the poached pears, peel the pears, leaving the stems on. Rub the flesh with a clean scourer to create a smooth finish.

In a saucepan large enough to hold all the pears, combine the wine, sugar, water, cinnamon, honey, ginger and vanilla. Bring the mixture to a simmer over medium heat, stirring occasionally, until the honey has melted.

Add the pears, reduce the heat to low, and simmer for 25–30 minutes, turning occasionally, until tender. If the pears are small, reduce the cooking time by 5 minutes.

Remove the pears from the liquid, transfer to a plate and leave to cool completely. They can be stored in the fridge while you finish the other preparations.

For the chocolate nests, place a slab of granite or marble or a heavy tray in the freezer, preferably overnight.

In a microwave-safe plastic bowl, heat the chocolate in the microwave on high in 30-second increments, stirring in between, until just melted.

Continued overleaf >

< Continued from previous page

FOR BEST RESULTS

> If you don't have a piece of portable stone, you can make the chocolate nests by piping the tempered chocolate in individual circles on a sheet of baking paper. When the chocolate sets, you can stack the chocolate circles to create the nest.

> As every pear is different, you can use a small knife to periodically test them while they are simmering to ensure you achieve a soft, tender consistency.

FIX IT

> If the ganache looks grainy just after you've made it, try whisking it vigorously. If it doesn't come together, boil another 2 tablespoons of cream, then add it to the ganache and whisk again.

NEXT LEVEL

> For an extra hit of alcohol, you can add 30 ml (1 fl oz) of William pear liqueur to the ganache after all the ingredients have been combined.

Transfer the melted chocolate to a snaplock bag or piping bag and cut a very small tip off the end.

Place the frozen stone or tray on a tea towel on your work surface. Pipe lines of chocolate, about 20–30 cm (8–12 inches) long and the thickness of spaghetti, onto the frozen stone. Lift the piped chocolate when set but still flexible, and twist it to create a nest that will fit the base of the pears. The best way to do this is to take a cup or mug that is slightly bigger than the base of your pear, freeze it, then place it on the frozen stone and wrap your chocolate around it to create your nest.

Leave the chocolate to set on the stone for up to 10 minutes before storing in an airtight container at room temperature.

To assemble, remove the core of each pear from its base, leaving the stem intact. Do this by turning the pear upside down and using a small knife to cut out the centre without removing the whole base.

Transfer half the prepared ganache to a piping bag fitted with a 1 cm (½ inch) plain piping nozzle. Fill the cavities in the base of the pears with ganache.

Set the pears aside in the fridge.

In a microwave-safe plastic bowl, melt the remaining ginger–chocolate ganache in the microwave on high, gently stirring with a spatula at 20-second intervals to avoid incorporating air, until completely melted but not hot.

Place the pears on a wire cooling rack with a tray underneath.

Pour the ganache over the pears. Leave them to sit for 2 minutes to allow the excess glaze to drip off. Using the stem, lift each pear slightly so the base is still in contact with the wire rack and twist it on the rack to remove any excess glaze from the base.

Place the prepared chocolate nests on serving plates. Top each with a pear just before serving.

The chocolate ganache can be made up to 2 weeks in advance and stored in an airtight container at room temperature below 25°C (77°F). The pears can be poached in advance and stored in an airtight container in the fridge for up to 2 days before filling and glazing.

CHAPTER 3

Playful, Quirky, Out-of-the-mould

Rocky Road Chocolate Cake

ROCKY ROAD CHOCOLATE CAKE

200 g (7 oz) whole eggs

115 g (4 oz) caster (superfine) sugar

2 vanilla beans, split lengthways
   and seeds scraped

95 g (3¼ oz) plain (all-purpose)
   flour

20 g (¾ oz) Dutch-process
   cocoa powder

½ teaspoon salt

20 g (¾ oz) unsalted butter, melted

30 g (1 oz) marshmallows, chopped

45 g (1½ oz) good-quality milk
   chocolate, roughly chopped

35 g (1¼ oz) roasted salted
   peanuts, roughly chopped

60 g (2¼ oz) fresh raspberries

CHOCOLATE GANACHE

200 ml (7 fl oz) thickened
   (whipping) cream

250 g (9 oz) good-quality milk
   chocolate

TO FINISH

45 g (1½ oz) good-quality milk
   chocolate, roughly chopped

30 g (1 oz) marshmallows, chopped

25 g (1 oz) roasted salted peanuts,
   roughly chopped

60 g (2¼ oz) fresh raspberries

Simply irresistible. This beauty is covered in luscious chocolate ganache and crowned with a halo of fresh raspberries, peanuts, marshmallows and milk chocolate. The inside of the cake is also studded with rocky road surprises. It's so much more than just another chocolate cake.

To make the cake, preheat the oven to 170°C (325°F) fan-forced.

Grease an 18 cm (7 inch) round cake tin.

Whisk the eggs, sugar and vanilla seeds in the bowl of a stand mixer with a whisk attachment on high speed for approximately 5 minutes, until light and fluffy.

To check whether the mixture is ready, lift the whisk and drizzle the mixture back onto itself. If it sits on top without immediately sinking back into the rest of the mixture, it is ready.

Sift the flour, cocoa powder and salt, then gradually add to the whisked egg mixture.

Mix a small amount of the batter into the melted butter, then fold all the butter into the batter to incorporate.

Add the marshmallows, chocolate, peanuts and raspberries and gently fold them through until evenly distributed.

Transfer the mixture to the prepared cake tin and bake for 30–35 minutes or until a skewer inserted into the centre comes out clean.

Leave to cool completely at room temperature.

For the chocolate ganache, heat the cream in a saucepan over medium heat and bring to the boil.

Put the chocolate in a bowl.

Pour the hot cream over the chocolate and whisk until the chocolate is completely melted and incorporated.

Cover with plastic wrap touching the surface of the ganache and leave to cool at room temperature for 2 hours, until it thickens to a spreadable consistency.

Continued overleaf >

< Continued from previous page

FOR BEST RESULTS

> Place the eggs in a bowl of body temperature water and leave for 10 minutes to warm them before making the cake. Gently move the eggs around as they warm. This will create better volume when whisking.

NEXT LEVEL

> For added glamour, replace the marshmallows on top with edible flowers.

Spread the chocolate ganache on top of the cake.

Arrange the chopped chocolate, marshmallows, peanuts and raspberries to form a halo around the top of the ganache.

The cake is best eaten within a few days of baking and served at room temperature. Store the undecorated cake in the fridge for up to 4 days. The cake can be made up to 4 weeks in advance and frozen. After the ganache and decoration are added, the cake can be stored for up to 3 days.

Hot Chocolate Churros with Choc–Marshmallow Dipping Sauce

CHOC–MARSHMALLOW SAUCE

125 g (4½ oz) good-quality
  dark chocolate
120 ml (4 fl oz) thickened
  (whipping) cream
150 g (5½ oz) marshmallows
15 g (½ oz) unsalted butter

CHOCOLATE CHURROS

240 ml (8 fl oz) water
300 g (10½ oz) caster (superfine)
  sugar, plus 2 teaspoons
50 g (1¾ oz) salted butter
115 g (4 oz) plain
  (all-purpose) flour
10 g (¼ oz) Dutch-process
  cocoa powder
100 g (3½ oz) whole eggs
1 litre (35 fl oz) canola oil,
  for deep-frying
½ teaspoon ground cinnamon

Churros, but make them chocolate. It's one thing to dip these moreish Spanish doughnuts in chocolate, but another entirely to work the chocolate into the doughnuts themselves. For the dipping sauce, think thick, fudgy, marshmallowy goodness. This wickedly decadent experience is one you'll want to repeat again and again.

To make the choc–marshmallow sauce, place the chocolate in a microwave-safe plastic bowl, then heat in the microwave on high in 30-second increments, stirring after each burst of heat, until the chocolate is completely melted.

Heat the cream in a saucepan over medium heat and bring to the boil.

Reduce the heat to low and add the marshmallows and butter to the hot cream, stirring until completely melted and combined.

Remove from the heat and combine with the melted chocolate. To avoid burning the chocolate, the sauce can be reheated when ready to serve, or kept warm over a very low heat.

For the chocolate churros, combine the water, the 2 teaspoons of caster sugar and the butter in a saucepan over medium heat and bring to the boil.

Add the flour and cocoa powder and stir vigorously to form a smooth dough.

Transfer the dough to the bowl of a stand mixer with a paddle attachment.

In a separate bowl, lightly break up the eggs with a fork.

Gradually add the eggs to the dough while mixing on medium speed until completely incorporated and the dough is smooth and shiny.

Transfer the dough to a piping bag fitted with a 1.2 cm (½ inch) star piping nozzle.

In a large heavy-based saucepan, heat the oil to 180°C (350°F).

Continued overleaf >

FOR BEST RESULTS

> These are best served hot, so ensure you make the sauce first.

> Test one churro in the oil first before cooking the whole batch to ensure the oil is at the correct temperature. If the oil is too hot, the churro will be uncooked on the inside, and if it is not hot enough, the churro will absorb some of the oil.

Meanwhile, in a separate bowl, combine the remaining sugar and the cinnamon, then set aside.

Pipe lengths of the dough over the hot oil and carefully snip them with kitchen scissors, allowing the dough to fall gently into the hot oil.

Fry for 4–5 minutes, until cooked through.

Carefully remove the churros with metal tongs and place on a plate lined with paper towel to absorb the excess oil.

While hot, toss the churros in the cinnamon sugar.

Serve immediately with the sauce.

The dough can be made and placed in a piping bag up to a day before frying. Once fried, the churros are best served immediately with freshly made chocolate sauce. The sauce is best enjoyed on the day it is made but can be stored in an airtight container in the fridge for up to 1 week.

Eton Mess with White Chocolate Chantilly & Strawberries

MERINGUE

60 g (2¼ oz) egg whites, at room
   temperature
pinch of cream of tartar
70 g (2½ oz) caster (superfine)
   sugar
65 g (2¼ oz) pure icing
   (confectioners') sugar

WHITE CHOCOLATE CHANTILLY

130 g (4½ oz) good-quality
   white chocolate
320 ml (11 fl oz) thickened
   (whipping) cream
20 g (¾ oz) liquid glucose
½ teaspoon vanilla bean paste

TO FINISH

300 g (10½ oz) fresh
   strawberries, quartered
40 g (1½ oz) pure icing
   (confectioners') sugar

Gaze into each glass to see a marvellous medley of flavours and textures. Sweet, light-as-a-feather meringue, with just the right amount of crispness. Thick, luscious, cold and creamy white chocolate chantilly. Fragrant fresh strawberries that create a syrupy goodness to seep into each element. This is definitely a dessert that you'll have on regular rotation.

To make the meringue, preheat the oven to 120°C (235°F).

Whisk the egg whites and cream of tartar until they reach firm peaks, then gradually add the caster and icing sugars. Continue whisking until the sugars have completely dissolved.

Spread the meringue out approximately 2 cm (¾ inch) thick over a baking tray lined with baking paper.

Bake the meringue for approximately 1½ hours or until crunchy.

Leave to cool, then store in an airtight container at room temperature until required.

For the white chocolate chantilly, put the chocolate in a bowl.

Combine 190 ml (6½ fl oz) of the cream, the glucose and the vanilla in a saucepan over medium heat and bring to the boil.

Pour the hot mixture over the white chocolate and whisk until the chocolate is completely melted and incorporated.

Whisk in the remaining cream, mixing until combined.

Cover with plastic wrap touching the surface of the chantilly and place in the fridge for a minimum of 6 hours. Alternatively, you can transfer to a tray lined with plastic wrap and place in the fridge for 2½ hours.

Whip the chilled chantilly until it reaches piping consistency.

Mix three-quarters of the strawberries with the icing sugar and leave to sit for 30–60 minutes.

To assemble, break up the prepared meringue and divide one-third of it among four 390 ml (13¾ fl oz) glasses.

Continued overleaf >

FOR BEST RESULTS

> Keep an eye on the meringue while baking. If it begins to colour, lower the temperature of the oven to keep it white.

> Note that while the longer you soak the strawberries, the more sauce you will create, the strawberries will also become dryer. Test the texture before keeping the strawberries in the sauce. If needed, strain them out of the sauce and replace them with fresh strawberries.

FIX IT

> If you overwhip the white chocolate chantilly, fold through some chilled cream to bring it back to a creamy consistency.

NEXT LEVEL

> For an added wow factor, assemble the Eton mess in one large trifle-sized bowl, instead of individual smaller bowls.

Use half of the whipped chantilly to create a layer on top of the crushed meringue.

Divide half of the strawberry and sugar mixture among the four glasses to top the whipped chantilly.

Repeat with another layer each of meringue, chantilly and strawberries.

Top with the remaining meringue and the reserved unsoaked strawberries.

Eton mess is best served immediately after assembling. The meringue can be made a week in advance and wrapped in plastic wrap once it cools to keep it crunchy. If the meringue goes soft, you can place it in a 120°C (235°F) oven until it dries out again. The white chocolate chantilly can be made up to 3 days in advance and whipped on the same day you assemble the dessert.

Marshmallow & Chocolate Snowball Squares

SNOWBALL SQUARES

vegetable oil spray,
  for greasing
4½ gelatine sheets
  of any variety
bowl of chilled water,
  for soaking
140 ml (4½ fl oz) cold water
225 g (8 oz) caster (superfine)
  sugar
pinch of sea salt
1 teaspoon vanilla bean paste

TO FINISH

150 g (5½ oz) desiccated coconut
2 teaspoons Dutch-process
  cocoa powder
450 g (1 lb) good-quality
  milk chocolate

Home-made marshmallow trumps the store-bought kind every time. Spongy and soft – and in this case dipped in melted chocolate and dusted in cocoa and coconut – these are bound to become your favourite marshmallow treats. This go-to sweet can also be used to elevate your rocky road, s'mores and hot chocolate.

For the snowball squares, grease a 16 x 26 cm (6¼ x 10½ inch) slice (slab) tin with vegetable oil spray and line with baking paper before spraying with additional vegetable oil.

Soak the gelatine sheets in the bowl of chilled water for approximately 5 minutes. Gently squeeze to remove the excess water from the soaked gelatine sheets and place them in the bowl of a stand mixer with a whisk attachment, then add 80 ml (2½ fl oz) of the cold water.

In a saucepan over medium heat, combine the remaining cold water and the sugar and bring to the boil until the sugar has completely dissolved.

Begin whisking the gelatine on low speed, then pour the hot syrup into the mixer bowl, while continuing to whisk.

Add the salt and vanilla, then increase the speed to medium and continue whisking until the mixture is white and has doubled in volume, 10–15 minutes.

Pour the mixture into the prepared slice tin and spread into an even layer. Place a lightly greased sheet of baking paper on top.

Leave to set at room temperature for 4 hours, until firm enough to cut.

Using a lightly oiled knife, cut the marshmallow into 24 squares of approximately 4 cm (1½ inches).

In a bowl, combine the coconut and cocoa powder, then pour the mixture out onto a tray.

Temper the chocolate by placing it in a microwave-safe plastic bowl and heating it in the microwave on high in 30-second increments, stirring in between. Once you have 50% solids and

FIX IT

> If the marshmallow starts to set in your mixer bowl, gently heat the outside of the bowl with a hair dryer, while continuing to whisk, until the mixture softens.

NEXT LEVEL

> The marshmallow can also be piped onto a greased tray to create domes.

50% liquid, stir vigorously until the solids have completely melted. If you have some resistant buttons, gently heat the chocolate with a hair dryer while stirring, until melted.

Using a fork, dip each marshmallow square in the tempered chocolate, then place it on the coconut mixture. Before the chocolate sets, scoop up the coconut mixture and sprinkle it over the square to coat evenly.

Place the snowball squares on a baking tray lined with baking paper and leave to set at room temperature.

The snowball squares can be made up to 3 weeks in advance and stored in an airtight container at room temperature below 25°C (77°F).

Moreish Fluffy Chocolate Marshmallow Knots

130 g (4½ oz) caster (superfine)
sugar, plus extra for holding
the tubes

80 ml (2½ fl oz) water

15 g (½ oz) powdered gelatine

145 g (5 oz) honey

60 g (2¼ oz) liquid glucose

135 g (4¾ oz) good-quality dark
chocolate

100 g (3½ oz) cornflour
(cornstarch)

100 g (3½ oz) pure icing
(confectioners') sugar

Soft, sweet and so much fun, these twisted bundles of fluffy marshmallow goodness are the stuff of dreams. They are great with a hot chocolate on a cold day ... if the kids don't eat them all first. For a simplified, but equally delicious variation, spoon dollops of the marshmallow onto greased sheets of baking paper.

Roll six sheets of baking paper into tubes, approximately 2 cm (¾ inch) in diameter, and secure with tape.

Pour a thin layer of extra caster sugar into a jug and set aside.

Pour 30 ml (1 fl oz) of the water into a small bowl, sprinkle the gelatine over the top and leave to sit for a few minutes. (The gelatine will absorb the water and create a firm paste.)

Place 85 g (3 oz) of the honey in the bowl of a stand mixer with a whisk attachment.

In a saucepan over medium heat, combine the caster sugar, the remaining honey, the remaining water and the glucose and heat to 113°C (235°F).

Once the syrup has reached temperature, pour it over the honey and start whisking on medium speed.

Heat the gelatine mixture in the microwave on high in 10-second increments until melted.

Add the melted gelatine to the mixer bowl and continue to whisk.

In a microwave-safe plastic bowl, heat the chocolate in the microwave on high in 30-second increments until melted, stirring in between each burst of heat.

Add the melted chocolate to the mixer bowl. Continue whisking until completely incorporated and the mixture has thickened but is still warm.

Immediately transfer the marshmallow mixture to a piping bag fitted with a plain piping nozzle small enough to fit into the baking-paper tubes.

Continued overleaf >

FOR BEST RESULTS

> Ensure the tape is wrapped all the way around so that it sticks to itself. Tape does not stick to baking paper.

> It takes 12 hours for the marshmallows to fully set. You can speed up the process by placing them in the fridge.

> When removing the marshmallows from the baking-paper tubes, keep in mind that the marshmallow will melt if it is too hot. If the marshmallow becomes too soft, place it back in the fridge to firm up before trying again with a little less heat.

NEXT LEVEL

> For an extra chocolatey hit, replace the cornflour with cocoa powder. You can also dust off the excess powder coating and cut the marshmallow strips before dipping in chocolate.

Pipe the marshmallow into the prepared tubes until it comes out the other end. Immediately stand the tubes upright in the jug of sugar – if the marshmallow cools too much it will become too firm to pipe into the tubes.

Leave to set for 2–3 hours at room temperature.

Combine the cornflour and icing sugar in a bowl, then sift them over a tray lined with baking paper.

To remove the marshmallows from the tubes, cut the tape and unroll the baking paper until the marshmallow is exposed. Heat the back of the paper with a hair dryer and shake gently until the marshmallow falls out. Let it drop into the cornflour mixture and roll each tube until it is well coated. This will prevent the marshmallow from sticking.

Cut into individual pieces – the size depending on how big you want the knots to be – and carefully tie each piece into a knot.

While still in the paper, these will keep for up to 4 weeks at room temperature. Once unmoulded, they will keep for a week in an airtight container.

Speckled Eggs with Three Types of Chocolate

1.3 kg (3 lb) good-quality white chocolate
⅓ teaspoon pink oil-soluble colour powder, or alternative colour of your choice
300 g (10½ oz) good-quality dark chocolate, roughly chopped
300 g (10½ oz) good-quality milk chocolate, roughly chopped
bowl of chilled water, for polishing

There are regular celebration eggs, and then there are these … a sensational medley of white, dark and milk chocolate specks scattered through stunning pink chocolate eggs. Polished to granite perfection, they look spectacular and taste even better. They make an incomparable centrepiece for the holiday table or an unforgettable gift. Either way, you will certainly make a lasting impression.

Use cotton wool to polish six half egg chocolate mould cavities, 12 cm (4½ inches) long.

Place a large sheet of baking paper on your work surface to catch any chocolate while creating the eggs.

Temper 1 kg (2 lb 4 oz) of the white chocolate by placing it in a microwave-safe plastic bowl and heating it in the microwave on high in 30-second increments, stirring in between. Once you have 50% solids and 50% liquid, stir vigorously until the solids have completely melted. If you have some resistant buttons, you can gently heat the chocolate with a hair dryer, while stirring, until melted.

Sift the pink colour powder over the tempered chocolate and stir to incorporate.

Mix the chopped-up pieces of the remaining white chocolate, and the milk and dark chocolate through the tempered chocolate.

Fill the egg moulds with the chocolate mixture, then tap the moulds on the work surface to dislodge any air bubbles.

Turn the mould upside down over the baking paper and tap the side of the mould with the handle of a metal scraper to create the egg shell. Be careful not to make the shell too thin (no less than 3 mm/⅛ inch).

Scrape the surface of the mould clean with the scraper or a palette knife while still holding it upside down.

Turn the mould over and ensure the top surface of the mould is also scraped clean.

FIX IT

> If the egg is not coming out of the mould, place it back in the fridge for a further 20 minutes. If you are still having trouble unmoulding, place it in the freezer for 20 minutes as a last resort. As tempting as it is, do not use any sharp implements to get the chocolate out as you will permanently damage the chocolate mould.

NEXT LEVEL

> These celebration eggs can be made with any combination of colours. Colour white chocolate by sifting in oil-soluble colour powder and mixing. Spread it out over baking paper and leave to set. Chop it into small pieces and use it as a coloured stone.

> Add flavour and crunch by mixing some roughly chopped roasted nuts into the chocolate (although the surface of the egg will not be as smooth).

Place the mould, chocolate side down, on a clean sheet of baking paper and leave to sit at room temperature for 10 minutes.

Turn the mould over and scrape the top again.

Place in the fridge for 15–20 minutes to fully set and allow the chocolate to contract from the mould.

Preheat the oven to 50°C (120°F) fan-forced and place a baking tray in the oven to warm up.

Carefully unmould the chocolate shells by gently tapping them out onto the work surface.

Slightly melt the edges of the egg halves on the warm tray, then join them together.

Slightly melt the base of the eggs on the warm tray to create a flat surface so that the eggs can stand upright.

Wet a clean, lint-free cloth with warm water and wipe the outside of the eggs to reveal the granite finish. Keep rinsing the cloth with more warm water as required.

Rinse the cloth thoroughly, then dip it in a bowl of iced water. Use the cold cloth to buff the surface of the eggs until they have a sheen. Continue dipping the cloth in the cold water as required.

The eggs can be made weeks in advance and wrapped in cellophane or stored in an airtight container.

These chocolate eggs, if well stored, will keep for up to 3 months at room temperature below 25°C (77°F).

FOR BEST RESULTS

> This technique can be used to make eggs of any size.

> The technique can be used with just two types of chocolate.

> The moulds can get heavy once filled with chocolate, so it's helpful to have an extra pair of hands to hold the mould while you are filling and tapping out the excess chocolate.

Pictured overleaf >

Chocolate Ganache Lollipops

CHOCOLATE GANACHE

100 ml (3½ fl oz) thickened
    (whipping) cream
350 g (12 oz) good-quality milk
    chocolate (33% cocoa)
50 g (1¾ oz) salted butter,
    at room temperature, cubed

TO ASSEMBLE

35 lollipop sticks

TO FINISH

600 g (1 lb 5 oz) good-quality
    milk chocolate (33% cocoa)

Delish on a stick. Experience the wonder of these fudgy ganache pops, chocolate-dunked and decorated with chocolate shavings for bonus texture and taste. You'll love the snap of the coating and the melt-in-the-mouth centre. Want to spice things up? Try adding some cinnamon or chilli powder to the ganache. Start these a day ahead to allow the ganache time to set.

To make the chocolate ganache, heat the cream in a saucepan over medium heat and bring to the boil.

Meanwhile, place the milk chocolate in a microwave-safe plastic bowl and heat in the microwave on high in 30-second increments, stirring in between, until you have 50% solids and 50% liquid.

Once the cream has come to the boil, pour it over the chocolate and whisk until the chocolate is completely melted and incorporated. Add the butter, a cube at a time, whisking after each addition until completely incorporated. Cover with plastic wrap touching the surface of the ganache and set aside at room temperature for 4 hours or until firm enough to pipe.

Transfer the ganache to a piping bag fitted with a 1.5 cm (⅝ inch) plain piping tube.

Line a tray with baking paper, securing the corners of the paper to the tray with a small amount of ganache.

Pipe 2.5 cm (1 inch) balls of ganache onto the baking paper.

Insert a lollipop stick in the centre of each ganache ball, ensuring the stick is pointing straight up. If the sticks do not hold in the ganache, allow the ganache balls to firm up slightly before inserting the sticks. Leave to sit at room temperature overnight.

Temper the chocolate by placing it in a microwave-safe plastic bowl and heating it in the microwave on high in 30-second increments, stirring in between. Once you have 50% solids and 50% liquid, stir vigorously until the solids have completely melted. If you have some resistant buttons, gently heat the chocolate with a hair dryer while stirring until they melt.

Pour one-quarter of the tempered chocolate onto a stone work surface (or stone slab) and immediately spread the chocolate into a thin layer with an offset palette knife. Continue to work the chocolate back and forth a few times. Once the chocolate is set

FOR BEST RESULTS

> You can speed up the setting process by placing the ganache in the fridge for about 30 minutes or until firm.

NEXT LEVEL

> Mix it up and make these lollipops into truffles. Use a toothpick to dip the truffles in the tempered chocolate.

to the touch, scrape it off the stone with a kitchen knife to create chocolate shavings. (Alternatively, you can scrape the back of a block of chocolate with a sharp knife to create shavings.) Set the shavings aside on a baking tray lined with baking paper and repeat until you have about 150 g (5½ oz) of shavings.

Reheat the remaining chocolate, if required, and dip the ganache lollipops in the tempered chocolate, one at a time. Let any excess chocolate drip off, then place the lollipops, with the sticks facing up, on the tray of chocolate shavings until set.

Once set, store any remaining chocolate in an airtight container for future use. The lollipops can be made up to 2 weeks in advance and stored in an airtight container at room temperature below 25°C (77°F).

Chocolate Tuile Tacos with Berries & Coconut Cream

TUILE

80 g (2¾ oz) unsalted butter,
   at room temperature
80 g (2¾ oz) pure icing
   (confectioners') sugar
75 g (2½ oz) plain
   (all-purpose) flour
15 g (½ oz) Dutch-process
   cocoa powder
50 g (1¾ oz) egg whites

COCONUT CREAM

250 g (9 oz) coconut cream
25 g (1 oz) liquid glucose
150 g (5½ oz) good-quality
   white chocolate
375 ml (13 fl oz) thickened
   (whipping) cream, chilled
50 g (1¾ oz) desiccated coconut

TO FINISH

300 g (10½ oz) fresh raspberries
300 g (10½ oz) fresh blueberries
250 g (9 oz) fresh strawberries,
   chopped
mint leaves, for garnishing
pure icing (confectioners') sugar,
   for dusting

This sweet taco look-alike is spot on for summer entertaining. There's nothing quite like the crisp snap of the tuile taco shell. Let the invigorating taste of summer wash over you with every bite. Fill the tacos with fresh berries and velvety coconut cream, or whatever flavours take your fancy.

To make the tuile, preheat the oven to 170°C (325°F) fan-forced.

Combine the butter and icing sugar in a bowl and mix by hand until smooth.

Sift in the flour and cocoa powder and lastly add the egg whites. Mix until the ingredients just come together as a smooth paste.

Create a stencil from an ice-cream lid or similar piece of plastic, by cutting and discarding a disc, 10 cm (4 inches) in diameter, out of the centre. You will be left with a ring of plastic with a hole in the middle.

Place the stencil on a baking tray lined with baking paper and spread a heaped tablespoon of the tuille mixture over the exposed baking paper in the middle of the stencil. Remove the stencil and repeat the process so that you have two discs on the tray.

Bake for 8–10 minutes.

Working quickly, lift the tuile while it's still hot and form it into a taco shape by folding it over a narrow rolling pin, then place a piece of scrunched foil in the centre to hold the shape while storing.

Repeat with the remaining tuile batter until you have created six taco shells.

Once cooled, store in an airtight container.

For the coconut cream, combine the coconut cream and glucose in a small saucepan over medium heat and bring to the boil.

Put the chocolate in a bowl.

Pour the hot liquid over the white chocolate and whisk until completely melted and combined.

Add the chilled cream and the coconut and mix to combine.

Continued overleaf >

FOR BEST RESULTS

> Do a test taco to determine the correct baking time for your tuiles. It can be difficult to tell whether chocolate products are baked enough as you can't rely on colour as an indicator. The baking time may vary depending on whether you've spread your tuile thicker or thinner than mine.

FIX IT

> If the second tuile disc cools and becomes too firm while you're forming the first into a taco, simply place it back in the oven for 2 minutes to soften again.

NEXT LEVEL

> For a more chocolatey hit, fill the tuile tacos with chocolate custard and berries, rather than coconut cream.

Cover with plastic wrap touching the surface and chill in the fridge for a minimum of 4 hours.

Whip the chilled coconut cream until it reaches piping consistency, about 2–3 minutes.

To assemble, transfer the whipped coconut cream to a piping bag fitted with a 1 cm (½ inch) plain piping nozzle and pipe it into the base of the tuile shells, filling them approximately one-third of the way. Alternatively, you can spoon the coconut cream into the shells.

Scatter the berries on top, followed by another few dollops of coconut cream.

Garnish with some additional berries and mint leaves, then dust with icing sugar.

Assemble just before serving like a traditional taco.

The coconut cream can be made up to 3 days in advance and whipped when you are ready to assemble. The taco shells are best made the same day and stored in an airtight container until you are ready to assemble.

White Chocolate & Blueberry Crumble Dessert with Cream Cheese Filling

WHITE CHOCOLATE TUBES

300 g (10½ oz) good-quality
  white chocolate

CREAM CHEESE FILLING

200 g (7 oz) cream cheese

30 g (1 oz) caster (superfine) sugar

100 ml (3½ fl oz) thick
  (double) cream

30 ml (1 fl oz) fresh lemon juice

1 teaspoon vanilla extract

pinch of sea salt

TO FINISH

150 g (5½ oz) fresh blueberries

2 store-bought good-quality
  shortbread biscuits, crumbled

mint leaves, for garnishing

Expect a feast in the form of textures and flavours. The sweet snap of white chocolate, the luscious cream cheese filling with hints of lemon and vanilla, the textured buttery crumble and the burst of blueberries. This is a restaurant-worthy dessert that's not as tricky as it looks. It's the dessert you've been waiting for.

To make the white chocolate tubes, make four tubes from baking paper, 5 cm (2 inches) in diameter, and secure with tape.

Scrunch some foil and place it inside the tubes to help the baking paper maintain its shape. (You will be piping chocolate onto the outside of the tubes.)

Lay the tubes on a sheet of baking paper, then place a teaspoon in each end of the tubes to ensure they won't move.

Temper the chocolate by placing it in a microwave-safe plastic bowl and heating it in the microwave on high in 30-second increments, stirring in between. Once you have 50% solids and 50% liquid, stir vigorously until the solids have completely melted. If you have some resistant buttons, gently heat the chocolate with a hair dryer while stirring until they melt.

Transfer the tempered chocolate to a piping bag, or snaplock bag with the corner snipped off, and pipe down the centre of each tube, allowing the chocolate to drip down the sides while trying to avoid the drips reaching the baking paper.

Place in the fridge for no more than 5 minutes, then store at room temperature until required.

For the cream cheese filling, mix the cream cheese and sugar until soft. Add the cream, lemon juice, vanilla and salt and mix to combine.

Place in the fridge until ready to serve.

Transfer the cream cheese filling to a piping bag fitted with a plain piping nozzle, approximately 1 cm (½ inch) in diameter.

Gently slide the baking paper out of the chocolate tubes.

FOR BEST RESULTS

> Ensure the tape is wrapped all the way around so that it sticks to itself. Tape does not stick to baking paper.

FIX IT

> If you are not happy with the shape of your chocolate tubes, wait for the chocolate to set, then re-temper it and start again.

Ensuring the drips are facing upwards, place a chocolate tube on a serving plate and secure it to the plate with a couple of dots of the cream cheese filling.

Pipe the cream cheese filling along the inside of the chocolate tube, then pipe some additional blobs of filling onto the plate.

Arrange the fresh blueberries and shortbread crumble over the piped cream cheese filling.

Lastly, garnish with fresh mint.

The chocolate for the tubes can be made up to 4 weeks in advance and stored in an airtight container at room temperature below 25°C (77°F). The cream cheese filling can be made 24 hours in advance and stored in the fridge. Stir until smooth before transferring it to a piping bag. You can assemble the dessert an hour before serving.

Chocolate Cream & Raspberry Jam Choux Sliders

CHOUX PASTRY BASE

vegetable oil spray or butter,
  for greasing
70 g (2½ oz) plain (all-purpose)
  flour, sifted, plus extra for dusting
65 ml (2¼ fl oz) full-cream milk
65 ml (2¼ fl oz) water
pinch of salt
5 g (⅛ oz) caster (superfine) sugar
45 g (1½ oz) unsalted butter
130 g (4½ oz) whole eggs
15 g (½ oz) sesame seeds

RASPBERRY JAM

140 g (5 oz) fresh or frozen
  raspberries
115 g (4 oz) caster (superfine) sugar
30 g (1 oz) liquid glucose

CHOCOLATE CREAM

245 ml (8½ fl oz) full-cream milk
½ teaspoon vanilla bean paste
10 g (¼ oz) custard powder or
  cornflour (cornstarch)
50 g (1¾ oz) caster (superfine) sugar
95 g (3¼ oz) egg yolks
135 g (4¾ oz) good-quality
  dark chocolate
70 g (2½ oz) unsalted butter,
  cubed

CHOCOLATE COATING

250 g (9 oz) good-quality milk
  chocolate
35 ml (1¼ fl oz) grapeseed oil
40 g (1½ oz) roasted salted
  peanuts, roughly chopped

These little beauties are a moreish mouthful of chocolate cream, jam and classic choux. They're irresistibly bite-sized and the fact that they look like mini burger buns just makes them even sweeter. With just the right amount of quirkiness, these chocolate sliders are the ultimate eating experience, bound to surprise your unsuspecting guests.

To make the choux pastry base, preheat the oven to 130°C (250°F) fan-forced. Prepare a baking tray by lightly greasing it with vegetable oil spray, then lightly dusting with flour.

Combine the milk, water, salt, sugar and butter in a medium saucepan over medium heat and bring to the boil.

Once boiling, remove from the heat and add the sifted flour. Stir vigorously and return to the heat. Continue stirring until the mixture comes together as a dough, has a light oily sheen on the surface and begins to come away from the side of the saucepan.

Remove from the heat and transfer the mixture to the bowl of a stand mixer with a paddle attachment.

In a bowl, break up the eggs with a fork.

Begin mixing the dough on low–medium speed and gradually add small amounts of the egg at a time, allowing it to completely incorporate after each addition. You may not need to add all the egg, so test the mixture regularly to ensure it reaches the correct consistency. To test the consistency, take a dessertspoonful of the mixture and hold it on its side: if the mixture slides off the spoon very slowly, it is ready.

Transfer the choux pastry to a piping bag fitted with a 1.2 cm (½ inch) plain piping nozzle.

Pipe rounds, 4.5 cm (1¾ inches) in diameter, onto the prepared tray, approximately 4 cm (1½ inches) apart.

Sprinkle the surface of each choux puff with sesame seeds.

Continued overleaf >

TO FINISH

small block good-quality
 white chocolate
mint leaves

Bake for 15 minutes, then increase the temperature to 150°C (300°F) and bake for a further 15 minutes. Lastly, increase the temperature to 170°C (325°F) and bake for a further 5 minutes, until the pastry is firm and dark golden brown. Do not open the oven door during the baking process.

Once baked, turn the oven off, open the door to release the steam and continue to dry out the choux for a few minutes. (This recipe makes a few extra choux buns. They can be wrapped in airtight packaging and stored in the freezer.)

To make the raspberry jam, place the raspberries, sugar and glucose in a saucepan over medium heat and bring to the boil, while stirring. Heat until it reaches 106°C (223°F). If you don't have a thermometer, test the jam by placing a small amount on a chilled plate – this will give you an idea of what the consistency will be once set. You want to achieve a soft jam consistency.

Transfer the jam to a bowl and cover with plastic wrap touching the surface.

Allow to cool at room temperature before storing in the fridge.

To make the chocolate cream, combine the milk and vanilla in a medium saucepan over medium heat and bring to the boil.

Meanwhile, place the custard powder and sugar in a separate bowl and whisk by hand to combine. Add the egg yolks and whisk to create a paste.

Pour the boiled milk over the egg mixture and whisk to combine. Transfer the mixture back to the saucepan and whisk over medium heat while it comes back to the boil. Remove from the heat and transfer to a bowl.

Add the dark chocolate and whisk until completely melted and combined.

Add the butter, one piece at a time, and whisk to incorporate.

Cover the bowl with plastic wrap touching the surface of the chocolate cream and place in the fridge for a minimum of 1 hour.

Slice the choux buns in half.

Transfer the chocolate cream into a piping bag fitted with a 1 cm (½ inch) plain piping nozzle.

Pipe the chocolate cream into the base of the choux buns and then pipe a second layer on top so it is raised above the pastry, replicating a burger patty.

Place the choux bases in the fridge for 20–30 minutes.

FOR BEST RESULTS

> Once the choux buns are piped, flick some water onto the tray before placing in the oven. This will create steam and give the choux a better lift.

> Dip your finger in water and gently tap down any peaks on the choux pastry before baking.

FIX IT

> If the cooked choux begins to soften, simply place it back in a 140°C (275°F) oven for 10–15 minutes to dry out.

> If the choux pastry didn't rise when baked, it is either because the mixture wasn't cooked enough once the flour was added, there was too much egg added, or it was taken out of the oven too soon. The buns can be dried out in the oven, cut and used, but they will be smaller.

Prepare the chocolate coating just before assembling the sliders.

Temper the chocolate by placing it in a microwave-safe plastic bowl and heating it in the microwave on high in 30-second increments, stirring in between. Once you have 50% solids and 50% liquid, stir vigorously until the solids have completely melted. If you have some resistant buttons, gently heat the chocolate with a hair dryer while stirring, until they melt.

Add the grapeseed oil and nuts to the tempered chocolate and mix to combine. Use immediately.

To assemble, remove the choux buns from the fridge and dip the top of the 'burger patty' chocolate cream in the prepared chocolate coating, ensuring you do not coat the choux pastry.

Heat the white chocolate block in a microwave-safe plastic bowl in the microwave on high for 10–15 seconds at a time, until slightly softened, then grate directly onto the chocolate-coated base to replicate grated cheese. If the chocolate doesn't resemble grated cheese it may need another 10 seconds in the microwave before grating.

Top with a drizzle of raspberry jam and some mint leaves, and lastly the choux pastry top.

These are best made and eaten the same day. The raspberry jam can be stored in the fridge for 1 month, as can the grated white chocolate. The chocolate cream can be made 3 days in advance and stored in the fridge.

The choux buns can be frozen raw or baked for up to 4 weeks. If frozen raw, leave them to thaw on the tray at room temperature or in the fridge before baking.

Chocolate & Coconut Truffle Swirl Popsicles

COCONUT TRUFFLE GANACHE

175 g (6 oz) good-quality
   white chocolate
65 ml (2 fl oz) coconut milk
50 g (1¾ oz) desiccated coconut

CHOCOLATE SWIRL COATING

1.6 kg (3 lb 8 oz) good-quality
   white chocolate
1 teaspoon orange oil-soluble
   colour powder
1 teaspoon pink or red oil-soluble
   colour powder

TO ASSEMBLE

25 lollipop sticks

Enchantingly whimsical, these coconut truffle swirl pops are filled with tongue-tingling sweet white chocolate and coconut ganache. A pretty chocolate pirouette of colours encases the mouthwatering insides to create a striking dessert. And to think these masterpieces are made with just a handful of ingredients! Start them a day ahead to allow the ganache time to set.

To make the coconut truffle ganache, place the chocolate in a microwave-safe plastic bowl and heat in the microwave on high in 30-second increments until it is 50% melted.

Heat the coconut milk in a saucepan over medium heat and bring to the boil.

Pour the hot coconut milk over the chocolate and whisk until the chocolate is completely melted and incorporated.

Add the desiccated coconut and whisk until incorporated.

Cover with plastic wrap touching the surface of the ganache. Leave to firm at room temperature overnight.

Take teaspoonfuls of the ganache and roll it into balls, then place them on a baking tray lined with baking paper.

Place in the fridge for 20 minutes, then leave them to come to room temperature before dipping.

For the chocolate swirl coating, temper the chocolate by placing it in a microwave-safe plastic bowl and heating in the microwave on high in 30-second increments, stirring in between. Once you have 50% solids and 50% liquid, stir vigorously until the solids have completely melted. If you have some resistant buttons, gently heat the chocolate with a hair dryer while stirring until they melt.

Dip the end of the lollipop sticks in the tempered chocolate, then press them into the prepared ganache balls.

Transfer approximately two-thirds of the tempered chocolate to a medium jug or small bowl and set aside. This chocolate will not be coloured.

Continued overleaf >

FOR BEST RESULTS

> Test whether the lollipop sticks will be securely inserted into the polystyrene or lollipop stand before you place them in the ganache balls. If required, use a pencil sharpener on the lollipop stick to ensure it can be inserted into the polystyrene.

> Don't start tempering the chocolate until your work surface is set up with everything you need.

> Warm each bowl and jug with a hair dryer before transferring the tempered chocolate into them.

Evenly divide the remaining chocolate between two bowls. Sift the orange colour powder into one bowl and the pink or red colour powder into the other. Stir well to colour the chocolate.

Transfer the coloured chocolates to separate snaplock bags and cut a small tip off the corner of each bag.

Pipe a grid pattern, using one colour at a time, on top of the white chocolate.

Dip a lollipop in the chocolate, twisting it as you pull it out.

Gently shake the lollipop over a sheet of baking paper to remove any excess chocolate, then hang it upside down, pressed into an elevated piece of polystyrene (suspend a sheet of polystyrene on two canisters or similar approximately 25–30 cm/10–12 inches high) or use a lollipop stand.

Repeat this process with the remaining lollipops, ensuring each new lollipop is dipped into the chocolate in an area that still has the grid pattern.

When the chocolate needs to be reheated, scrape the coloured section off the top, then gently heat with a hair dryer and repeat the process until all the lollipops have been dipped.

Leave the lollipops to set at room temperature for a minimum of 10 minutes.

These can be made up to 2 weeks in advance and stored in an airtight container at room temperature below 25°C (77°F).

CHAPTER 4

Creamy, Smooth, Chilled

Fresh Strawberry & Creamy White Chocolate Semifreddo

STRAWBERRY SYRUP

70 g (2½ oz) caster (superfine) sugar

300 g (10½ oz) fresh strawberries, roughly chopped

2 vanilla beans, split lengthways and seeds scraped

SEMIFREDDO

100 g (3½ oz) good-quality white chocolate

65 ml (2¼ fl oz) thick (double) cream

150 ml (5 fl oz) thickened (whipping) cream

1 vanilla bean, split lengthways and seeds scraped

65 g (2¼ oz) Greek-style yoghurt

strawberry syrup, above

TO FINISH

300 g (10½ oz) fresh strawberries, finely diced

A refreshing and impeccably harmonised creation. Semifreddo translates to 'semi frozen', and these creamy delights will be just starting to melt as you dig in. Big on flavour and low on effort, they're a win-win. The white chocolate is perfectly balanced by the yoghurt and brought together with fruity notes from strawberry-spiked syrup.

To make the strawberry syrup, place the sugar, strawberries and vanilla seeds in a heatproof bowl over a saucepan of simmering water and heat for 30 minutes.

Carefully remove from the heat, then strain the syrup and discard the strawberries. Evenly divide the syrup between two bowls and set aside to cool at room temperature.

For the semifreddo, place six egg rings on a tray, then line each ring with a paper muffin case. To do this, press the paper cases down to create a flat base and allow the edges to go up the sides of the egg rings.

Put the white chocolate in a bowl.

Heat the thick cream in a saucepan over medium heat and bring to the boil.

Pour the cream over the chocolate and whisk until the chocolate is completely melted and incorporated. Set aside to cool slightly.

Meanwhile, semi-whip the thickened cream with the vanilla seeds, until it has some body but still collapses.

Gently fold the yoghurt through the semi-whipped cream until there are no lumps remaining.

Fold the cream and yoghurt mixture through the chocolate mixture in three batches.

Add one bowl of the cooled strawberry syrup and gently fold it through until incorporated and completely smooth.

Pour the mixture into the prepared paper cases and gently smooth the surface with the back of a spoon. Place in the freezer for 4 hours.

FOR BEST RESULTS

> Be gentle with the paper muffin cases to ensure you keep the fluted pattern on the sides.

> The longer you leave the strawberries to soak with the sugar, the more juice you will create.

Pour the remaining strawberry syrup over the frozen semifreddo before returning to the freezer for a minimum of 2 hours.

Unmould the semifreddo and place on a serving plate. Garnish by arranging the diced strawberries in a line across, or over half of, the surface.

The strawberry syrup can be made up to 3 days in advance and stored in the fridge. Keep the strawberries in for as long as possible and only strain before assembling. The semifreddo can be made up to 4 weeks in advance – simply store in an airtight container in the freezer once frozen. When you remove it from the freezer, it needs to be served immediately.

Tiramisu with White Chocolate Ice Cream & Coffee Soak

WHITE CHOCOLATE NO-CHURN ICE CREAM

500 ml (17 fl oz) thickened (whipping) cream
50 g (1¾ oz) mascarpone
1 teaspoon vanilla bean paste
150 g (5½ oz) good-quality white chocolate
395 ml (13¾ fl oz) sweetened condensed milk
½ teaspoon sea salt

COFFEE SOAK

300 ml (10½ fl oz) water
390 g (13¾ oz) caster (superfine) sugar
30 g (1 oz) Dutch-process cocoa powder
90 ml (3 fl oz) espresso coffee
120 ml (4 fl oz) Marsala wine (you can omit the alcohol, if you prefer)

TO ASSEMBLE

200 g (7 oz) sponge fingers (savoiardi biscuits/lady fingers)
Dutch-process cocoa powder, for dusting

Prepare yourself for classic tiramisu vibes in ice cream form. Utterly creamy white chocolate ice cream with a traditional hint of mascarpone, sponge fingers soaked in fragrant Marsala-spiked coffee, dusted with rich cocoa powder. Layer upon layer of mouthwatering bliss. For perfect dinner party portions, prepare the recipe as eight individual serves.

To make the ice cream, combine 150 ml (5 fl oz) of the cream, the mascarpone and vanilla in a saucepan over medium heat and bring to the boil.

Put the white chocolate in a bowl.

Pour the hot mixture over the chocolate and whisk until it is completely melted and incorporated.

Add the remaining cream and whisk to combine.

Cover with plastic wrap touching the surface of the mixture and place in the fridge for a minimum of 5 hours.

Add the condensed milk and salt to the chilled white chocolate mixture and whisk until it forms soft peaks. This can be done in a stand mixer with a whisk attachment or with hand-held electric beaters. Ensure the cream mixture doesn't sit out of the fridge before whipping as it needs to be very cold to prevent the mixture from splitting.

Place in the freezer for up to 1 hour while you prepare the coffee soak.

Combine the water and sugar in a saucepan over high heat and bring to the boil.

Once the sugar has completely dissolved, remove from the heat and add the cocoa powder, coffee and Marsala. Mix to combine. Leave to cool at room temperature.

Dip half the sponge fingers in the coffee soak until they feel well soaked. You can test one by breaking it in half to see how far the coffee mixture goes in. You are aiming for it to soak the sponge finger almost to the centre.

Continued overleaf >

140

< *Continued from previous page*

FOR BEST RESULTS
> Ensure that the sponge fingers are well soaked when assembling.

FIX IT
> If you overwhip the ice cream base, simply fold through a small amount of chilled cream.

Arrange the sponge fingers over the base of a 23 cm (9 inch) square dish or baking tin.

Spread half of the ice cream mixture over the sponge fingers to create an even layer.

Repeat with another layer of coffee-soaked sponge fingers and ice cream mixture.

Generously dust the surface with cocoa powder, then place in the freezer for a minimum of 4 hours.

Store in the freezer for up to 4 weeks and serve frozen. Take the tiramisu out of the freezer and place it in the fridge for 30 minutes before serving, to soften it slightly.

The Simplest Raspberry & Cream Tart with White Chocolate Curls

CRUMB BASE

250 g (9 oz) digestive (sweet wholemeal) biscuits

120 g (4¼ oz) unsalted butter, melted

½ teaspoon ground cinnamon

CREAM TOPPING

300 ml (10½ fl oz) thick (double) cream

50 g (1¾ oz) caster (superfine) sugar

TO ASSEMBLE

375 g (13 oz) fresh raspberries

100–200 g (3½–7 oz) block good-quality white chocolate

FIX IT

> If the base is too crumbly, place it back in a bowl and add a little more melted butter.

> The tart base softens quickly when sitting at room temperature. Place it back in the fridge to firm it up.

When I say simple, I mean it. This spectacularly easy tart not only looks divine but tastes sensational. It's all of the yum and wow with none of the fuss. Beautiful, fresh raspberries are the key. However, you can use the crumb base and cream as a foundation for *your* favourite toppings. How about peaches or sliced banana?

To make the crumb base, in a food processor, blitz the biscuits to create a fine crumb.

Combine the biscuit crumbs, melted butter and cinnamon and mix until it reaches a wet sand consistency.

Press the mixture into the base of a greased 23 cm (9 inch) fluted flan (tart) tin with a removable base.

Place in the fridge to set for a minimum of 30 minutes.

Once the base has set, remove it from the tin, place it on a flat serving plate and return to the fridge.

For the cream topping, whisk the cream and sugar until the mixture reaches a spreadable consistency.

Spread the whipped cream filling in an even layer on top of the biscuit base.

Cover the cream with the fresh raspberries.

Place the block of white chocolate on an overturned microwave-safe plastic bowl and heat in the microwave on high for 10–15 seconds, until it is soft enough to create big curls with a vegetable peeler.

Arrange the chocolate curls on top of the tart.

Make the crumb base up to 4 days in advance. Up to a day before serving, top with the raspberries and cream, then finish with the white chocolate just before serving.

Lamington Ice Creams with Raspberry & Coconut

WHITE CHOCOLATE NO-CHURN ICE CREAM

285 ml (9¾ fl oz) thickened
(whipping) cream

½ teaspoon vanilla bean paste

75 g (2½ oz) good-quality
white chocolate

200 ml (7 fl oz) sweetened
condensed milk

125 g (4½ oz) fresh raspberries

GANACHE COATING

100 g (3½ oz) desiccated coconut

300 g (10½ oz) good-quality dark
chocolate

420 ml (14½ fl oz) thickened
(whipping) cream

TO ASSEMBLE

16 popsicle sticks

Seductively creamy, cool and sweet. Home-made ice cream is given a lamington spin with hints of fresh raspberry, a chocolate shell and loads of coconut. Don't have ice cream moulds? This frozen treat is just as wickedly delicious made in a tray. Simply slather the luscious ganache coating over the ice cream and add a satisfying sprinkling of coconut.

To make the ice cream, combine 100 ml (3½ fl oz) of the cream and the vanilla in a saucepan over medium heat and bring to the boil.

Place the white chocolate in the bowl of a stand mixer with a whisk attachment.

Pour the boiled cream over the chocolate and whisk until the chocolate is completely melted and incorporated.

Add the remaining cream and whisk to combine.

Cover with plastic wrap touching the surface of the mixture, then place in the fridge for a minimum of 5 hours.

Once the cream base mixture has chilled, place the condensed milk in the bowl of a stand mixer with a whisk attachment.

Pour the chilled chocolate cream mixture over the condensed milk, add the raspberries and whip on high speed until it forms soft peaks.

Divide the mixture among 16 mini ice cream silicone moulds, then insert a popsicle stick into each ice cream.

Place the ice creams in the freezer to set for at least 6 hours, preferably overnight.

For the ganache coating, tip the coconut into a bowl and set aside until required.

Once the ice creams are completely frozen, place the chocolate in a microwave-safe plastic bowl and melt in the microwave on high in 30-second increments until 50% melted.

Heat the cream in a saucepan over medium heat and bring to the boil.

Continued overleaf >

FOR BEST RESULTS

> These are best left in the freezer overnight before removing from the moulds. I used Silikomart Mini Classic Ice Cream Moulds.

> Left-over ganache coating can be frozen, then reheated and poured over ice cream or a dessert for an extra chocolate hit whenever you desire.

FIX IT

> The ice cream base whips very quickly so don't walk away from the mixer. If you do happen to overmix it slightly, gently fold through some chilled cream.

Pour the boiled cream over the chocolate and whisk until the chocolate is completely melted and incorporated.

Transfer the ganache to a tall jug or vase that is just wide enough to dip an ice cream into.

Dip each ice cream, one at a time, in the jug of ganache, then hold over the bowl of coconut. Scoop up the coconut and sprinkle it over the ice cream until all the ganache is coated. Alternatively, place the ganache-coated ice cream on top of the coconut and use a dessertspoon to scoop up the coconut and sprinkle it over the ice cream. Try not to move the ice cream too much while coating with coconut, as it can make the surface of the ice cream lumpy. Place the ice cream on a tray lined with baking paper and return to the freezer for a minimum of 1 hour before serving.

Store in the freezer for up to 4 weeks. Any left-over ganache coating can be frozen for up to 8 weeks.

Raspberry Lemonade & White Chocolate Mousse Pots

300 ml (10½ fl oz) thickened (whipping) cream

250 g (9 oz) fresh raspberries

200 ml (7 fl oz) good-quality store-bought raspberry lemonade

300 g (10½ oz) good-quality white chocolate

250 g (9 oz) chocolate ripple biscuits (or plain chocolate cookies), plus a few extra to garnish

FOR BEST RESULTS

> If making this recipe as one large trifle, set each layer slightly by placing it in the freezer before you add the next layer.

NEXT LEVEL

> Garnish with individual chocolate flower petals from my chocolate cheesecake tart recipe (see page 169).

> The raspberry lemonade can be replaced with more cream, then incorporated the same way. You may want to increase the raspberries if you do this.

The not-so-secret ingredient that makes this deliciously easy and airy mousse is good old-fashioned raspberry lemonade. It creates a wonderful, mellow raspberry flavour that contrasts with the dark chocolate crumb. Don't want to make individual desserts? Simply create this as one large, stunning trifle. It's a tremendous and trouble-free dessert to make, either way.

In the bowl of a stand mixer with a whisk attachment, combine the cream and 60 g (2¼ oz) of the fresh raspberries, then whisk on high speed to a semi-whipped consistency. Set aside in the fridge until required.

In a saucepan over high heat, bring the raspberry lemonade to the boil.

Put the white chocolate in a bowl.

Pour the hot lemonade over the chocolate and whisk until the chocolate is completely melted and incorporated.

Cool at room temperature for 30–40 minutes or until cool to the touch, stirring about every 10 minutes.

Fold the chilled raspberry cream through the chocolate base.

Crush the chocolate ripple biscuits to a rough crumb in a plastic bag using a rolling pin.

Place a layer of biscuit crumbs in the base of six 240 ml (8 fl oz) jars, then spoon a layer of mousse on top so that it fills the jars one-third of the way.

Repeat with another two layers of biscuits and mousse to fill the jars.

Leave to chill in the fridge for a minimum of 4 hours.

Before serving, garnish with broken chocolate ripple biscuits and fresh raspberries.

These pots can be made up to 3 days in advance and stored in the fridge. They are best served straight from the fridge.

Strawberry Trifle with White Chocolate Mousse

STRAWBERRY SOAK

500 g (1 lb 2 oz) fresh strawberries, chopped
200 g (7 oz) caster (superfine) sugar
50 ml (1½ fl oz) water
½ teaspoon vanilla bean paste

TO PREPARE THE DISH

500 g (1 lb 2 oz) fresh strawberries of varying sizes

WHITE CHOCOLATE MOUSSE

600 ml (21 fl oz) thickened (whipping) cream
1 teaspoon vanilla bean paste
380 g (13½ oz) good-quality white chocolate
400 ml (14 fl oz) thick (double) cream

TO ASSEMBLE

300 g (10½ oz) sponge fingers (savoiardi biscuits/lady fingers)
100–200 g (3½–7 oz) block good-quality milk chocolate
200 ml (7 fl oz) thick (double) cream
125 g (4½ oz) fresh strawberries, each cut into 8 thin wedges

Enter a world of strawberry syrup–soaked sponge, seductively sweet white chocolate mousse, and an abundance of fresh summery strawberries. The beauty of this knockout trifle comes from the varying shapes and sizes of the fresh strawberry slices. The best part is we're not aiming for perfect uniformity, which makes this simply stunning effect very easy to create.

To make the strawberry soak, place the strawberries, sugar, water and vanilla in a heatproof glass bowl.

Place the bowl on top of a saucepan of simmering water for 30 minutes, stirring occasionally.

Strain the syrup from the strawberries, then discard the strawberries. Set the syrup aside at room temperature.

To prepare the dish, slice the strawberries crossways into 5 mm (¼ inch) rounds.

Arrange the sliced strawberries around the inside of a 20 cm (8 inch) glass trifle dish, until they reach approximately 3 cm (1¼ inches) from the top (see photograph on page 156).

Chop the remaining strawberry slices and reserve them for the trifle assembly.

For the white chocolate mousse, combine the thickened cream and vanilla in a saucepan over medium heat and bring to the boil.

Put the white chocolate in a bowl.

Pour the hot cream over the chocolate and whisk until the chocolate is completely melted and incorporated.

Place the ganache in the fridge for 20–30 minutes, stirring regularly until cool to the touch and thickened.

Transfer the cooled ganache to a larger bowl and add the thick cream, one-third at a time, folding it through. This mixture needs to be used immediately after the thick cream is added.

FOR BEST RESULTS

> When assembling the trifle, make sure the sponge fingers are well soaked.

To assemble the trifle, one at a time, dip the sponge fingers in the strawberry soak and arrange them in two even layers over the base of the trifle dish.

Sprinkle half of the reserved chopped strawberries over the soaked sponge layer.

Pour half of the chocolate mousse into the dish, then place the trifle in the fridge for 20–30 minutes or until it has started to set slightly.

Grate some milk chocolate over the mousse layer.

Repeat with another layer of soaked sponge fingers, chopped strawberries and mousse.

Chill in the fridge for a minimum of 6 hours, preferably overnight.

Before serving, warm a tablespoon slightly with hot water and scoop the cream straight from the tub – it should hold its shape – onto the surface of the trifle. Just before serving, scatter the strawberry wedges on top of the cream.

The trifle can be stored in the fridge for up to 3 days. It can be made up to 2 days in advance and stored in the fridge to ensure it has the best appearance, but it can still be eaten for up to 3 days.

The strawberry mixture can be made in advance and stored in the fridge for up to 5 days. Leave the strawberries in until you are ready to assemble the trifle and the sugar will continue to draw juice out of them.

Pictured overleaf >

Opposite: Strawberry Trifle with White Chocolate Mousse   Above: Chocolate Cake Topped with Swiss Meringue Cloud

Chocolate Cake Topped with Swiss Meringue Cloud

CHOCOLATE CAKE

75 g (2½ oz) unsalted butter

205 g (7¼ oz) good-quality
   dark chocolate

65 g (2¼ oz) soft brown sugar

100 g (3½ oz) whole eggs

½ teaspoon vanilla bean paste

55 g (2 oz) plain (all-purpose) flour

¼ teaspoon baking powder

10 g (¼ oz) Dutch-process
   cocoa powder

pinch of salt

60 g (2¼ oz) egg whites, at room
   temperature

pinch of cream of tartar

65 g (2¼ oz) caster (superfine)
   sugar

50 g (1¾ oz) good-quality milk
   chocolate, finely chopped

SWISS MERINGUE

90 g (3¼ oz) egg whites, at room
   temperature

¼ teaspoon cream of tartar

200 g (7 oz) caster (superfine) sugar

TO FINISH

60 g (2¼ oz) fresh raspberries

The flavours of rich chocolate, sweet meringue and tart raspberries harmonise perfectly in this to-die-for tea party cake. Part silky Swiss meringue, part luscious chocolate cake, it's an all-star combo that's bound to impress. You will be looking for any excuse to make this one again and again.

To make the chocolate cake, preheat the oven to 170°C (325°F) fan-forced. Grease and line a 21 x 11 cm (8¼ x 4¼ inch) cake tin.

Combine the butter and 155 g (5½ oz) of the dark chocolate in a microwave-safe plastic bowl. Heat in the microwave on high in 30-second increments until completely melted and combined. Or place the chocolate and butter in a saucepan and stir over low heat until completely melted and combined.

Place the brown sugar, eggs and vanilla in a bowl and whisk by hand to combine.

Sift the flour, baking powder and cocoa powder and salt into a bowl, then add to the egg mixture and fold it through to make the cake batter.

In a stand mixer with a whisk attachment, or using hand-held electric beaters, whisk the egg whites and cream of tartar. Once the egg whites reach medium peaks, gradually add the caster sugar, then continue whisking for a further minute to dissolve the sugar and stabilise the meringue.

Fold the melted butter and chocolate mixture through the cake batter.

Add the meringue to the cake batter in three stages and gently fold it through each time.

Lastly, add the finely chopped milk chocolate and remaining dark chocolate and gently fold them through.

Transfer the mixture to the prepared cake tin and bake for 35–40 minutes, until a skewer inserted into the centre comes out clean.

Remove from the oven and leave to cool at room temperature, then remove from the tin.

158

FOR BEST RESULTS

> Note that you will always get more volume out of your egg whites if you whisk them when they are at room temperature rather than straight from the fridge.

> When toasting the meringue topping, hold the blowtorch at least 10 cm (4 inches) from the surface of the meringue. Move the blowtorch continuously over the surface. Be especially careful of the peaks as they will burn easily.

NEXT LEVEL

> Layer it up! Bake thinner layers of cake and sandwich them with the meringue, finishing with a layer of meringue on top.

> This cake can be made in a different-shaped tin. Try a heart-shaped tin for Valentine's Day.

For the Swiss meringue, combine the egg whites, cream of tartar and sugar in a heatproof bowl placed over a saucepan of simmering water. Heat, while whisking, until the mixture reaches 60°C (140°F).

Remove from the heat and whisk in a stand mixer with a whisk attachment, or using hand-held electric beaters, until the meringue cools and reaches firm peaks.

Spoon the meringue on top of the cooled cake.

Use an offset palette knife or the back of a spoon to spread the meringue over the surface, creating some texture and peaks.

With the help of a kitchen blowtorch, toast the surface of the meringue.

To finish, serve the cake with a side of fresh raspberries.

The cake is best enjoyed at room temperature.

Store at room temperature for 4–5 days.

Pictured overleaf >

The Ultimate Silky Chocolate Flan

CHOCOLATE CUSTARD FILLING

100 g (3½ oz) whole eggs

75 g (2½ oz) caster (superfine) sugar

35 g (1¼ oz) cornflour (cornstarch)

250 ml (9 fl oz) thickened (whipping) cream

250 ml (9 fl oz) full-cream milk

75 g (2½ oz) good-quality dark chocolate (57% cocoa)

ROUGH PUFF PASTRY

170 g (6 oz) unsalted butter, cold

175 g (6 oz) baker's flour, plus extra for dusting

¼ teaspoon salt

60–70 ml (2–2¼ fl oz) iced water

If you've never tried the silky, chocolatey sensation that is a custard flan, you've been missing out. A rough puff pastry and borderline addictive chocolate filling puts this tart in a league of its own. For the most indulgent taste and texture, bring the flan out of the fridge 20 minutes before serving. Trust me, it makes a big difference.

To make the custard filling, place the eggs, sugar and cornflour in a bowl and whisk by hand until there are no lumps remaining.

Add the cream and whisk to combine.

Heat the milk in a saucepan over medium heat until just below boiling point.

Put the dark chocolate in a bowl.

Slowly pour the hot milk over the egg mixture while whisking.

Transfer the mixture back to the saucepan. Whisk continuously over medium heat until the custard begins to thicken.

Immediately pour the custard over the chocolate and whisk until the chocolate is completely melted and incorporated.

Cover with plastic wrap touching the surface of the custard and leave to cool completely in the fridge.

For the rough puff pastry, grate the cold butter. If the butter begins to soften, place it back in the fridge before continuing.

Place the grated butter, baker's flour and salt in a bowl.

Gradually add the iced water while mixing by hand, until the ingredients just come together as a dough with visible pieces of butter remaining. You may not need all the water.

On a floured work surface, roll the dough out into a rectangle, approximately 35 x 20 cm (14 x 8 inches).

From a short edge, fold the dough one-third of the way in on itself, then fold the opposite side on top.

Wrap in plastic wrap and chill in the fridge for 30 minutes.

Continued overleaf >

< Continued from previous page

FOR BEST RESULTS

> Ensure the pastry base is completely baked through before adding the custard. Every oven is different, so the pastry may require a longer baking time.

FIX IT

> If you notice any holes or gaps in the pastry, patch them up with your rolled pastry scraps.

Return the dough to your work surface, roll it out into a rectangle, then fold it as above.

Rotate the dough 90 degrees and repeat the rolling and folding process again.

Wrap the dough with plastic wrap and place in the fridge for 30 minutes.

Preheat the oven to 220°C (425°F) fan-forced.

Place a round cake ring, 16 cm (6¼ inches) in diameter and 4 cm (1½ inches) high, on a baking tray lined with baking paper.

Roll out the chilled dough into a rectangle and fold it one final time as above.

Finally, roll out the dough to approximately 3 mm (⅛ inch) thick and pierce it all over with a fork to ensure it does not rise.

Cut a disc approximately 26 cm (10½ inches) in diameter out of the dough and use it to line the cake ring. Do not trim the excess dough at the top.

Line the dough with scrunched then flattened baking paper, and fill with uncooked rice. Bake for 20 minutes. (This is called blind baking.)

Remove the paper and rice and bake for a further 15 minutes, until light golden. Leave the oven on.

Leave the pastry base to cool slightly before using a serrated knife to trim any excess pastry from the top.

Whisk the chilled chocolate custard filling until smooth.

Fill the prepared pastry case with the custard. Use a spoon or spatula to smooth it out, ensuring it is level with the top of the pastry.

Bake on the top rack of the oven for 10–15 minutes, until the custard begins to form a skin and starts to colour.

Remove the flan from the oven and leave to cool slightly.

Leave to cool completely in the fridge. Ensure the custard filling is chilled and set before cutting.

Store in the fridge for up to 3 days.

Semifreddo Peanut Butter Double-choc Mousse Bombs

PEANUT BUTTER MOUSSE

225 ml (7¾ fl oz) thickened (whipping) cream, chilled

100 g (3½ oz) caster (superfine) sugar

50 ml (1½ fl oz) water

¼ teaspoon vanilla bean paste

125 g (4½ oz) crunchy peanut butter

50 g (1¾ oz) good-quality white chocolate

40 g (1½ oz) unsalted butter, cubed

½ teaspoon sea salt

TO FINISH

400 g (14 oz) good-quality milk chocolate

60 g (2¼ oz) roasted salted peanuts, roughly chopped

FOR BEST RESULTS

> The chocolate in this recipe does not need to be tempered, as it will set when frozen.

> To reduce the sweetness, you can dip the semifreddo bombs in dark chocolate.

Frozen peanut butter mousse with a crisp chocolate and peanut shell – a bit like a chocolate-topped ice cream but even better. The sweet and salty flavour combination unites beautifully with the creamy, slightly crunchy texture to make for a truly sensory treat.

For the peanut butter mousse, cut out six 30 cm (12 inch) squares of plastic wrap and use them to line six small cups. Set aside.

Semi-whip the cream until it has some body but still collapses. Cover with plastic wrap and set aside in the fridge until required.

In a saucepan over high heat, bring the sugar, water and vanilla to the boil.

Place the peanut butter and white chocolate in a bowl, then pour the boiling sugar mixture on top, whisking to combine.

Add the butter and salt and whisk to combine. Leave to cool to body temperature before adding the semi-whipped cream and folding it in.

Divide the semifreddo among the six prepared cups.

Pinch the top of the plastic wrap and twist it to create a teardrop shape, then place the cups in the freezer for a minimum of 4 hours.

Place the milk chocolate in a microwave-safe plastic bowl and heat in the microwave on high in 30-second increments until completely melted but not too hot, approximately 35°C (95°F).

Remove the semifreddo from the cups and remove the plastic wrap. Insert a skewer or toothpick into the bottom of each semifreddo and dip it in the melted chocolate.

Working quickly, sprinkle some chopped peanuts over the chocolate before it sets. Transfer to a plate or airtight container, remove the skewer and return the semifreddo to the freezer until ready to serve.

These can be made up to 4 weeks in advance and stored in the freezer in an airtight container once frozen. They need to be served straight from the freezer.

No-bake Triple Chocolate Cheesecake Tart with a Chocolate Flower

CHOCOLATE CRUMB BASE

200 g (7 oz) chocolate ripple biscuits
   (or plain chocolate cookies)
80 g (2¾ oz) unsalted butter,
   melted

CHEESECAKE FILLING

190 ml (6½ fl oz) thickened
   (whipping) cream
410 g (14½ oz) cream cheese,
   at room temperature, cubed
50 g (1¾ oz) caster (superfine)
   sugar
15 g (½ oz) pure icing
   (confectioners') sugar
½ teaspoon ground nutmeg
1 teaspoon vanilla bean paste
pinch of salt
1½ teaspoons lemon juice

CHOCOLATE GLAZE

95 ml (3¼ fl oz) thickened
   (whipping) cream
35 g (1¼ oz) liquid glucose
90 g (3¼ oz) good-quality
   dark chocolate
½ teaspoon vanilla extract

CHOCOLATE FLOWER GARNISH

250 g (9 oz) good-quality
   dark chocolate

We're talking chocolate-crumb base, creamy cheesecake and a glossy chocolate glaze. No baking required, but applause welcome. And the flower – delicate chocolate brushstrokes form enchanting petals that, when assembled, create an exquisite embellishment. The flower can also be made smaller or larger to garnish countless creations.

To make the chocolate crumb base, grease a fluted flan (tart) tin, 20 cm (8 inches) in diameter and 3.5 cm (1¼ inches) high, and line the base with baking paper.

Crush the biscuits in a food processor to a fine crumb.

In a bowl, mix the biscuit crumbs with the melted butter, then press into the base and side of the flan tin.

Place in the fridge until required.

For the cheesecake filling, in the bowl of a stand mixer with a whisk attachment, semi-whip the cream on medium speed until it has some body but still collapses. Set the cream aside in the fridge until required.

Change the whisk to a paddle attachment. Mix the cream cheese on medium speed until softened. Add the caster sugar, icing sugar, nutmeg, vanilla and salt, and continue to mix until smooth and creamy, scraping down the side of the bowl as required. Add the lemon juice and mix until incorporated.

Remove the bowl from the mixer, add the semi-whipped cream and gently fold it through.

Spoon the filling into the prepared tart shell and spread until smooth and even, ensuring there is enough space remaining for the chocolate glaze.

Place in the fridge to set for a minimum of 1 hour.

For the chocolate glaze, combine the cream and glucose in a saucepan over medium heat and bring to the boil.

Put the chocolate in a bowl.

Continued overleaf >

Pour the cream mixture over the chocolate and whisk until the chocolate is completely melted and incorporated. Add the vanilla and mix to combine.

Cover with plastic wrap touching the surface and leave to cool at room temperature.

For the chocolate flower garnish, cut five strips of baking paper, approximately 7 x 30 cm (2¾ x 12 inches).

Temper the chocolate by placing it in a microwave-safe plastic bowl and heating it in the microwave on high in 30-second increments, stirring in between. Once you have 50% solids and 50% liquid, stir vigorously until the solids have completely melted. If you have some resistant buttons, gently heat the chocolate with a hair dryer, while stirring, until melted.

To create individual petals, dip a dry pastry brush in the tempered chocolate, then brush it in a slightly curved line onto the baking paper strips.

Leave 10 petals flat on the work surface and slide 20 petals, on their baking paper, just to sit in the mouth of a wide jug to curve them as they set. Leave to set at room temperature before gently removing the baking paper.

Use a hair dryer to gently reheat the remaining chocolate, while stirring.

Place a teaspoonful of the chocolate in the centre of a 3 cm (1¼ inch) square piece of baking paper.

Create an outer layer of petals by arranging five of the flat petals in a circle so that each base is in contact with the melted teaspoonful of chocolate (or you can make the flower out of all curved petals).

Spoon some additional melted chocolate into the centre and arrange the remaining flat petals so that they sit in between the first layer.

To add the remaining petals, dip the back of each curved petal in the melted chocolate, then add them to the centre of the flower base until the flower is full.

Leave to set at room temperature. (The recipe allows enough to make additional petals to allow for breakages.)

To assemble, remove the cheesecake from the tin and transfer to a serving plate.

Heat the prepared glaze in the microwave on high, gently stirring at regular interviews, until just warm to the touch.

FOR BEST RESULTS

> I use the lid from a can of vegetable oil spray to press the biscuit crumb into the base of the tin.

> You can assemble the flower directly on the cake so you don't have to lift and transfer it.

FIX IT

> If the biscuit crumb is not compressing, put it back in the bowl and add a little more butter.

NEXT LEVEL

> This cake is lovely with fresh berries folded through the filling.

> For a striking look, use tempered white chocolate with some oil-soluble colour powder added for the chocolate flower.

> You can make the flower bigger by using a wider pastry brush.

Pour the glaze on top of the cheesecake. Any remaining glaze can be used when serving the tart.

Top the tart with the chocolate flower and serve.

The flower petals can be made and stored at room temperature below 25°C (77°F) for up to 4 weeks. The filled tart can be made up to 3 days in advance and stored in the fridge. Finish with the chocolate glaze and flower a few hours before serving and keep chilled until serving.

CHAPTER 5

Old-fashioned, Comfort, Classic

Toasty Chocolate Almond Croissants

CHOCOLATE ALMOND CREAM

60 g (2¼ oz) unsalted butter, softened

90 g (3¼ oz) caster (superfine) sugar

60 g (2¼ oz) whole eggs

90 g (3¼ oz) almond meal

10 g (¼ oz) Dutch-process cocoa powder

TO ASSEMBLE

120 ml (4 fl oz) water

160 g (5½ oz) caster (superfine) sugar

6 x day-old croissants

120 g (4¼ oz) flaked almonds

pure icing (confectioners') sugar, for dusting

FOR BEST RESULTS

> Keep an eye on the flaked almonds so they don't burn – they should turn a golden colour.

> Check that your croissants are made with butter and not vegetable fat for a better flavour.

NEXT LEVEL

> You can make these nut-free but equally delish if you replace the almond meal with ground sunflower seeds and the flaked almonds with whole sunflower seeds.

A fuss-free creation that brunch dreams are made of. Close your eyes and savour the experience of biting into this crisp, buttery goodness. These flavour-filled croissants pack a proper patisserie punch, minus the effort. The chocolate almond cream alone will have you reaching for a second. The shocking truth is, the older the croissants, the better results you'll get, with a satisfyingly crunchy exterior.

To make the chocolate almond cream, cream the butter and sugar in a stand mixer with a paddle attachment, mixing until there are no lumps of butter remaining.

Gradually add the eggs, while continuing to mix until incorporated. Scrape down the side of the bowl as required.

Add the almond meal and cocoa powder and mix to combine.

Preheat the oven to 170°C (325°F) fan-forced.

Combine the water and sugar in a saucepan over high heat and bring to the boil. Once the sugar has dissolved, remove from the heat and set aside.

Cut the croissants in half horizontally. Dip the cut sides in the prepared syrup before transferring them to a baking tray lined with baking paper.

Spread or pipe half of the chocolate almond cream onto the sugar-soaked bases, then top with the croissant tops.

Dip the top of the croissants in the syrup, pipe or spread the remaining almond cream on top, then finish with a generous sprinkle of the flaked almonds.

Bake for 20–25 minutes, until the almonds are toasted and golden brown.

Before serving, dust the surface of the croissants with icing sugar.

Before baking, you can store the croissants in the freezer for up to 8 weeks and bake them fresh once thawed. They are best stored at room temperature for up to 3 days.

Ginger Swirl Cake with White & Dark Chocolate Marbled Glaze

GINGER PREPARATION

225 g (8 oz) fresh ginger

700 ml (24 fl oz) water

300 g (10½ oz) caster (superfine)
  sugar

GINGER CAKE

235 g (8½ oz) unsalted butter

2 teaspoons plain
  (all-purpose) flour

200 g (7 oz) muscovado sugar

50 g (1¾ oz) black treacle

150 g (5½ oz) golden syrup
  (light treacle)

100 g (3½ oz) whole eggs,
  lightly beaten

300 ml (10½ fl oz) full-cream milk

ginger matchsticks, above, or
  220 g (7¾ oz) store-bought
  stem ginger slices cut into
  matchsticks

50 ml (1½ fl oz) ginger syrup,
  above, or 50 ml (1½ fl oz) syrup
  from store-bought stem ginger

365 g (12¾ oz) self-raising flour

1 teaspoon sea salt

3 teaspoons ground ginger

½ teaspoon ground cinnamon

½ teaspoon bicarbonate of soda
  (baking soda)

CHOCOLATE GLAZE

800 g (1 lb 12 oz) good-quality
  white chocolate

150 g (5½ oz) good-quality dark
  chocolate

100 ml (3½ fl oz) grapeseed oil

One of my all-time faves, this show stopper manages to taste every bit as good as it looks. The cake itself has an intricate flavour profile: bittersweet treacle notes and gorgeous hints of toffee, with a subtle hint of cinnamon spice. Please don't be intimidated by the marble glaze – the cake is brilliant with or without it.

Peel the ginger before thinly slicing into matchsticks.

Combine the water and ginger in a medium saucepan and simmer, with the lid on, for approximately 2½ hours, until the ginger is tender.

Strain the ginger over a bowl and reserve the liquid.

Pour 300 ml (10½ fl oz) of the ginger-infused water into a saucepan over high heat. If too much of the liquid evaporated during the simmering process, make up the difference by adding more water.

Add the sugar and bring to the boil.

Once the sugar has completely dissolved, add the strained ginger and simmer for 5 minutes. Remove from the heat and leave to cool at room temperature.

Once cool, store the ginger and syrup in an airtight container in the fridge until required. (If you do not wish to prepare the ginger for the cake, simply use store-bought stem ginger in syrup, cutting the ginger into fine matchsticks.)

For the cake, preheat the oven to 160°C (315°F) fan-forced.

Melt 15 g (½ oz) of the butter in a small saucepan over low heat. Brush the melted butter over the inside of a bundt tin, 22 cm (8½ inches) in diameter and 10 cm (4 inches) deep. Add the plain flour and rotate the tin until the inside is coated with flour, then tap out any excess flour and set aside.

In a clean saucepan over medium heat, combine the remaining butter, the sugar, treacle and golden syrup. Stir until the ingredients have melted and combined. Transfer the mixture to a bowl and leave to cool slightly at room temperature.

FOR BEST RESULTS

> When glazing, it's handy to have someone stand on the other side of the cake to make sure the glaze is covering the entire surface.

> Glaze the cake as quickly as possible so that the glaze sets as one piece where it overlaps. To buy some more time, gently warm the cake surface with a hair dryer so the chocolate will take longer to set.

NEXT LEVEL

> For an added pop of colour, you can replace some of the dark chocolate with additional white chocolate that you have coloured with oil-soluble colour powder. You still need a bit of the dark chocolate for contrast.

> The cake can be made in any shaped tin, but you may need to adjust the baking time.

Add the beaten eggs and milk and whisk to combine.

Add the ginger matchsticks, ginger syrup, self-raising flour, salt, ginger, cinnamon and bicarbonate of soda and gently fold them through.

Pour the cake batter into the prepared tin and bake for 40–45 minutes. The cake is ready when a skewer inserted into the centre comes out clean.

Leave the cake to sit at room temperature for 10 minutes before removing from the tin. Place the cake on a wire rack and leave to cool completely.

Once cool, wrap the cake in plastic wrap and place in the fridge for 3 hours, or overnight.

For the glaze, temper the white chocolate by placing it in a microwave-safe plastic bowl and heating it in the microwave on high in 30-second increments, stirring in between. Once you have 50% solids and 50% liquid, stir vigorously until the solids have completely melted. If you have some resistant buttons, you can gently heat the chocolate with a hair dryer, while stirring, until melted.

Repeat this tempering process with the dark chocolate in a separate bowl.

Add 80 ml (2½ fl oz) of the grapeseed oil to the white chocolate, and the remaining grapeseed oil to the dark chocolate, mixing to combine.

Transfer the chocolate mixtures to a jug, alternating the white and dark to create layers (see photo overleaf).

Place the chilled cake on a wire rack over a tray with sides and pour the glaze over the cake.

Using a sharp knife, trim the glaze from around the base of the cake before the chocolate becomes too firm.

Transfer the cake to a serving plate and place in the fridge for 2 hours before serving.

The ginger cake can be frozen for up to 8 weeks before it is glazed. Bring it back to room temperature before glazing. Store the glazed cake at room temperature for up to 5 days.

Pictured overleaf >

Chocolate Freckles with Sprinkles & Toasted Coconut

100 g (3½ oz) desiccated coconut

200 g (7 oz) good-quality
  milk chocolate

200 g (7 oz) hundreds and
  thousands (coloured round
  sprinkles)

It's hard to describe why the humble freckle – a classic Australian favourite – evokes such joy. There are hundreds (and thousands) of reasons to be giddy with excitement for the traditional colourful crunch, while lightly toasted coconut takes this childhood favourite to a whole new level. Don't make me choose. I love all my freckles equally.

Preheat the oven to 160°C (315°F) fan-forced.

Spread the coconut evenly over a baking tray lined with baking paper and bake for 2–3 minutes. Remove from the oven and stir, then bake for another 2–3 minutes, until golden brown. Leave to cool completely at room temperature.

Temper the chocolate by placing it in a microwave-safe plastic bowl and heating it in the microwave on high in 30-second increments, stirring in between. Once you have 50% solids and 50% liquid, stir vigorously until the solids have completely melted. If you have some resistant buttons, gently heat the chocolate with a hair dryer, while stirring, until melted.

Use a sheet of baking paper to line a tray with sides.

Transfer the tempered chocolate to a snaplock bag and cut a small tip off the corner. Pipe a few discs at a time, gently tapping the tray on the work surface to level out the chocolate, then sprinkle coconut over half of the chocolate discs and hundreds and thousands over the remaining discs. Repeat this process until all the chocolate is used.

Leave to set at room temperature, then remove any excess coconut and hundreds and thousands. If your room temperature is warm, place the freckles in the fridge for 10 minutes to set.

These are best stored in an airtight container at room temperature below 25°C (77°F) for up to 3 months.

FOR BEST RESULTS

> Stop your toppings going everywhere and collect them easily by covering a section of your work surface with plastic wrap, then place the tray you are piping onto on top.

NEXT LEVEL

> Rub a little edible gold lustre powder into the coconut before sprinkling it over the piped chocolate.

180

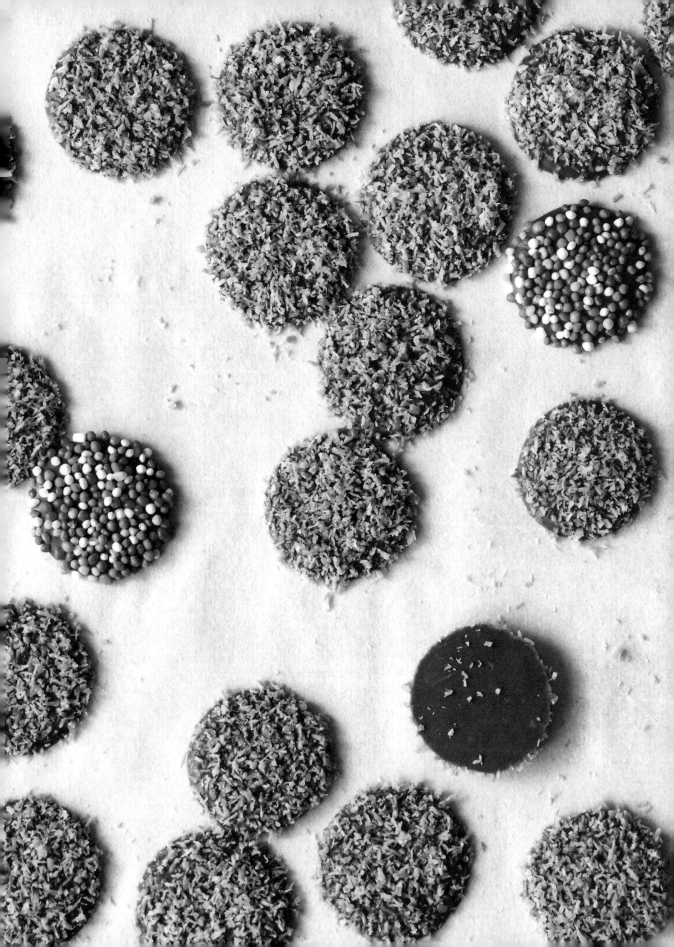

Comforting Glazed Marble Loaf Cake

MARBLE CAKE

200 g (7 oz) unsalted butter,
    softened
350 g (12 oz) caster (superfine)
    sugar
1 teaspoon vanilla extract
pinch of sea salt
200 g (7 oz) whole eggs,
    at room temperature
195 g (7 oz) plain
    (all-purpose) flour
1 teaspoon baking powder
90 ml (3 fl oz) full-cream milk
25 g (1 oz) Dutch-process
    cocoa powder

GLAZE

30 g (1 oz) unsalted butter
60 g (2¼ oz) caster (superfine)
    sugar
60 ml (2 fl oz) water
½ teaspoon vanilla extract

Never underestimate a simple cake. Marvel at the hypnotic vanilla and cocoa swirl of this light loaf cake's marbled centre. With an added touch of sweetness from the understated but seductive glaze, you'll be cutting a slice for afternoon tea, an after-dinner snack, and perhaps even a cheeky breakfast.

To make the marble cake, preheat the oven to 160°C (315°F) fan-forced. Grease a 21 x 11 cm (8¼ x 4¼ inch) loaf (bar) tin and line the base with baking paper. You can also use an 18–20 cm (7–8 inch) round or square tin.

In a stand mixer with a paddle attachment, beat the butter, sugar, vanilla and salt until light and fluffy, starting on medium speed and gradually building up to high speed – scrape the side of the bowl as required.

In a separate bowl, lightly whisk the eggs.

Gradually add the egg to the mixer, starting with just a dessertspoonful at a time. Mix well after each addition to prevent the cake mixture separating.

Weigh 180 g (6½ oz) of the mixture and set aside to create the chocolate batter. The remaining mixture will be used to create the vanilla batter.

Sift 160 g (5½ oz) of the flour with ¾ teaspoon of the baking powder, then gradually fold them through the vanilla portion of the butter mixture, alternating it with 70 ml (2¼ fl oz) of the milk and ending with the final flour addition. (This helps prevent the mixture separating.) Once all the flour is incorporated it is important to stop mixing, to prevent the cake becoming tough once baked.

Sift the remaining flour, with the cocoa powder and the remaining baking powder, then fold it through the reserved chocolate portion of the butter mixture, alternating it with the remaining milk.

Alternate spooning the two mixtures into the prepared loaf tin and zigzag the handle of a dessertspoon from one end of the batter to the other, to create marbled layers.

Continued overleaf >

FOR BEST RESULTS

> It's important to beat the butter and sugar really well, ensuring they are light and fluffy and the sugar is dissolved.

> Before starting the cake, warm the eggs to body temperature by placing them in a bowl over a water bath. Gently move the eggs around while they warm.

> When alternating adding flour and milk, always start with a bit of flour.

NEXT LEVEL

> For an extra layer of decadence, top with the ganache from my Rocky road chocolate cake (see page 97).

Bake for 55–60 minutes, until a skewer inserted into the centre comes out clean.

For the glaze, combine the butter, sugar, water and vanilla in a saucepan over medium heat and bring to the boil.

Simmer for 1 minute before brushing the glaze over the warm cake while It is still in the tin.

Once the cake has cooled, remove it from the tin.

The loaf can be frozen for up to 4 weeks, or stored at room temperature for no more than 5 days.

Chocolate, Vanilla & Raspberry Lamington Sponge

VANILLA & RASPBERRY SPONGE

200 g (7 oz) whole eggs

110 g (3¾ oz) caster (superfine) sugar

½ teaspoon vanilla bean paste

115 g (4 oz) plain (all-purpose) flour, sifted

pinch of salt

20 g (¾ oz) unsalted butter, melted

120 g (4¼ oz) fresh or frozen raspberries

COCOA SOAKING SYRUP

120 g (4¼ oz) caster (superfine) sugar

120 ml (4 fl oz) water

45 g (1½ oz) Dutch-process cocoa powder

20 g (¾ oz) raspberry jam

COCONUT COATING

125 g (4½ oz) desiccated coconut

20 g (¾ oz) Dutch-process cocoa powder

VANILLA CREAM

400 ml (14 fl oz) thickened (whipping) cream

50 g (1¾ oz) caster (superfine) sugar

½ teaspoon vanilla bean paste

TO ASSEMBLE

raspberry jam

good-quality block dark chocolate

125 g (4½ oz) fresh raspberries

An Australian icon, the humble lamington is elevated to centrepiece status. Tantalising raspberry-studded vanilla sponge is coated with cocoa-spiked syrup, then covered in chocolatey coconut. It's also loaded with fluffy whipped vanilla cream and raspberry jam and finally embellished with dark chocolate shavings and fresh raspberries.

To make the vanilla and raspberry sponge, preheat the oven to 165°C (320°F) fan-forced. Grease two 18 cm (7 inch) round cake tins.

Whisk the eggs, sugar and vanilla on high speed in the bowl of a stand mixer with a whisk attachment for approximately 5 minutes, until light and fluffy.

To check whether the egg mixture is ready, lift the whisk and drizzle the mixture back onto itself. If it sits on top without immediately sinking back into the rest of the mixture, it's ready.

Add the sifted flour and salt in three stages, gently folding them through the egg mixture.

Mix a small amount of the batter into the melted butter before folding all the butter through the batter.

Break up the raspberries slightly by hand, then gently fold them through the batter.

Divide the mixture evenly between the prepared cake tins.

Bake for 15–18 minutes, until the sponge bounces back when gently pressed.

Leave the sponges to sit at room temperature for 5 minutes before removing from the tins and cooling on a wire rack.

Once cool, wrap the sponges in plastic wrap and place in the freezer for a minimum of 40 minutes.

For the cocoa soaking syrup, combine the sugar, water, cocoa powder and jam in a saucepan over medium heat, and whisk to combine before bringing to the boil.

Remove from the heat and leave to cool at room temperature.

Continued overleaf >

FOR BEST RESULTS

> To help give your cake a lift, warm the eggs to body temperature by placing them in a bowl over a water bath. Gently move the eggs around while they warm up.

NEXT LEVEL

> To make this sweeter, omit the cocoa powder from the coconut coating.

> Add some additional height by layering three cakes instead of two. To do this, increase all the ingredient quantities by 50%.

> Garnish with individual chocolate petals, from my chocolate cheesecake tart recipe (see page 169), between the raspberries.

For the coconut coating, place the coconut and cocoa powder in a bowl and combine by rubbing together with your fingertips. Transfer to a flat tray and set aside until required.

For the vanilla cream, whisk the cream, sugar and vanilla until the mixture has a piping consistency.

Transfer the cream to a piping bag fitted with a 1.2 cm (½ inch) star piping nozzle.

If required, use a serrated knife to trim the top off the frozen sponge cakes to create a flat surface.

Using a pastry brush, brush the soaking syrup around the side of one of the frozen sponges, as well as around 1 cm (½ inch) of the top edge.

Using your hands, press the coconut coating onto the syrup-soaked sponge. Place on a serving plate.

Brush the side and top of the second layer of sponge cake with soaking syrup, then press the coconut coating onto the soaked surfaces. Set aside, unsoaked side down, until required.

Spread a layer of raspberry jam on top of the sponge on the serving plate.

Pipe a layer of vanilla cream over the jam in a shell pattern.

Sit the second layer of sponge, coconut-coated side up, on top of the piped cream.

Scrape a border through the coconut around the top of the cake, 1.5 cm (⅝ inch) from the edge.

Pipe the vanilla cream onto the border in a shell pattern.

Run a vegetable peeler along the side of the block of chocolate to create dark chocolate shavings.

Finish by garnishing the cake with the chocolate shavings and fresh raspberries.

The sponge cakes can be made up to 4 weeks in advance, then frozen. The cocoa soaking syrup can be made 2 days in advance. Once the cake is prepared, it can be stored in the fridge for up to 3 days.

Caramel Slice Topped with Milk Chocolate Ganache

BISCUIT BASE

125 g (4½ oz) unsalted butter,
　melted
200 g (7 oz) soft brown sugar
120 g (4¼ oz) plain (all-purpose)
　flour
50 g (1¾ oz) desiccated coconut
pinch of ground cinnamon
50 g (1¾ oz) good-quality milk
　chocolate, roughly chopped

CARAMEL FILLING

80 g (2¾ oz) unsalted butter,
　cubed
80 g (2¾ oz) soft brown sugar
1 teaspoon vanilla extract
395 ml (13¾ fl oz) sweetened
　condensed milk
90 g (3¼ oz) good-quality
　dark chocolate

GANACHE TOPPING

250 g (9 oz) good-quality
　milk chocolate
100 ml (3½ fl oz) thickened
　(whipping) cream
1 teaspoon vanilla extract
30 g (1 oz) liquid glucose
pinch of sea salt

Just when you think caramel slice (sometimes known as millionaire's shortbread) can't get any better, I bring you this new level of decadence. What makes this caramel slice so good? Chocolate, of course. Here you'll find it nestled in the biscuit base, humming in the caramel filling and crowning this slice in the form of a glossy ganache.

To make the biscuit base, preheat the oven to 160°C (315°F) fan-forced. Grease a slice (slab) tin, 27.5 x 17.5 cm (11 x 6¾ inches) and 3.5 cm (1¼ inches) high. Line the base and sides of the tin with baking paper and set aside until required.

Put the melted butter and brown sugar in a bowl and mix with a wooden spoon to combine. Add the flour, coconut and cinnamon. Continue to mix until the ingredients come together.

Add the milk chocolate and mix to combine.

Press the mixture into the base of the prepared baking tin to create an even layer.

Bake for 15 minutes.

Remove from the oven and set aside at room temperature.

Reduce the oven temperature to 140°C (275°F) fan-forced.

For the caramel filling, combine the butter, brown sugar and vanilla in a saucepan over medium heat.

Once the butter has melted and the sugar has completely dissolved, reduce the heat to low, add the condensed milk and whisk continuously until the mixture begins to simmer. Continuing to whisk, cook for a further 3 minutes until the mixture begins to thicken slightly.

Remove from the heat and add the dark chocolate. Mix until the chocolate is melted and incorporated into the caramel.

Pour the caramel filling over the biscuit base and spread to create an even layer.

Bake for approximately 25 minutes.

Continued overleaf >

190

NEXT LEVEL

> To add a little dazzle, rub some edible gold lustre dust into shaved or shredded coconut and sprinkle it on top of each bar.

Remove from the oven and leave the slice to cool completely at room temperature.

For the ganache topping, place the chocolate in a bowl.

Combine the cream, vanilla, glucose and salt in a saucepan over medium heat. Bring to the boil, then pour the mixture over the chocolate. Gently whisk until the chocolate is completely melted and incorporated into the other ingredients.

Pour the ganache over the cooled caramel layer and spread evenly. (For a less rich version, make the slice without the ganache topping.)

Place the slice in the fridge for 30 minutes to set.

Remove the caramel slice from the tin and cut it into 18 rectangles, approximately 9 x 2.8 cm (3½ x 1¼ inches).

Store the slice in an airtight container at room temperature for up to 2 weeks.

Lush Chocolate Berry Layer Cake with White Chocolate Chantilly Cream

CHOCOLATE SPONGE

200 g (7 oz) whole eggs, at room
   temperature
100 g (3½ oz) caster (superfine)
   sugar
1 tablespoon vanilla bean paste
95 g (3¼ oz) plain
   (all-purpose) flour
15 g (½ oz) Dutch-process
   cocoa powder
pinch of sea salt
20 g (¾ oz) unsalted butter, melted
60 g (2¼ oz) good-quality
   milk chocolate, chopped

WHITE CHOCOLATE CHANTILLY

330 ml (11¼ fl oz) thickened
   (whipping) cream
1 teaspoon vanilla bean paste
35 g (1¼ oz) liquid glucose
220 g (7¾ oz) good-quality
   white chocolate

TO FINISH

300 g (10½ oz) mixed fresh berries

This is a sensationally mouthwatering go-to for the warmer seasons with its sweet yet refreshing flavours. Light, airy and layered with white chocolate chantilly and ripe summer berries, this chocolate sponge is truly a classic. Pipe the cream on for a polished finish, or layer it on thick for a more rustic yet equally delightful look.

To make the chocolate sponge, preheat the oven to 165°C (320°F) fan-forced. Grease an 18 cm (7 inch) round cake tin.

Whisk the eggs, sugar and vanilla in the bowl of a stand mixer with a whisk attachment on high speed for approximately 5 minutes, until light and fluffy.

To check whether the egg mixture is ready, lift the whisk and drizzle the mixture back onto itself. If it sits on top without immediately sinking back into the rest of the mixture, it is ready.

Sift the flour, cocoa powder and salt into a bowl, then add it to the egg mixture and gently fold through.

Mix a small amount of the sponge batter into the melted butter before folding all the melted butter through the batter.

Add the milk chocolate and gently fold it through.

Transfer the mixture to the prepared cake tin and bake for 35–40 minutes, until a skewer inserted into the centre comes out clean.

Leave to cool completely at room temperature before removing the cake from the tin.

Once cooled, freeze the sponge for a minimum of 30 minutes, to make it easier to slice.

Using a serrated knife, slice the chocolate sponge into three even horizontal layers.

For the white chocolate chantilly, combine 220 ml (7¾ fl oz) of the cream, the vanilla and glucose in a saucepan over medium heat and bring to the boil.

Put the white chocolate in a bowl.

FOR BEST RESULTS

> Cutting the sponge from one side to the other can create uneven layers. Instead, make marks around the sponge where you will cut it and cut while turning the sponge until you reach the centre.

NEXT LEVEL

> Add some white chocolate curls, from my raspberry and cream tart recipe (see page 145), to the berries.

Pour the hot cream mixture over the chocolate and whisk until the chocolate is completely melted and incorporated. Add the remaining cream and whisk to combine.

Cover with plastic wrap touching the surface of the chantilly and place in the fridge for a minimum of 6 hours.

Whisk the white chocolate chantilly until it reaches piping consistency, then transfer to a piping bag fitted with an 8 mm (⅜ inch) star piping nozzle.

Place a layer of chocolate sponge on a serving plate and pipe one-third of the chantilly cream over the surface.

Scatter some berries over the chantilly cream.

Repeat with the second layer of sponge, chantilly and berries.

Add the final layer of sponge, pipe the remaining cream on top, then decorate the cake with the remaining berries.

The chocolate sponge can be made up to 4 weeks in advance and frozen. The white chocolate chantilly cream can be made the day before whipping. Once assembled, the cake will last 3 days in the fridge.

Pictured overleaf >

Decadent Six-layer Chocolate Cake with Milk Chocolate Curls

CHOCOLATE CAKE

vegetable oil spray, for greasing

420 g (15 oz) plain (all-purpose) flour

105 g (3½ oz) Dutch-process cocoa powder

15 g (½ oz) bicarbonate of soda (baking soda)

1 teaspoon baking powder

420 g (15 oz) caster (superfine) sugar

1 teaspoon salt

115 ml (3¾ fl oz) coconut oil or vegetable oil

100 g (3½ oz) whole eggs

120 ml (4 fl oz) buttermilk

1 teaspoon vanilla bean paste

120 ml (4 fl oz) hot water

DECADENT CHOCOLATE GANACHE

540 ml (18½ fl oz) thickened (whipping) cream

1 teaspoon vanilla bean paste

60 g (2¼ oz) liquid glucose

1.14 kg (2 lb 8 oz) good-quality milk chocolate

CHOCOLATE SOAK

100 ml (3½ fl oz) water

100 g (3½ oz) caster (superfine) sugar

1 teaspoon vanilla bean paste

1 tablespoon Dutch-process cocoa powder

MILK CHOCOLATE CURLS

250 g (9 oz) good-quality milk chocolate

The ultimate, most unashamed, elaborate display of chocolate. If I had to describe this cake in one word, it would be *lush*. Layers of lust-worthy chocolate cake brushed with an irresistible chocolate syrup, crowned with ganache and adorned with milk chocolate curls. This is truly chocolate royalty.

To make the chocolate cake, preheat the oven to 150°C (300°F). Grease two 18 cm (7 inch) round cake tins with vegetable oil spray, then line them with baking paper.

Sift the flour, cocoa powder, bicarbonate of soda and baking powder into a bowl, add the sugar and salt, then set aside.

In a stand mixer with a whisk attachment, beat the coconut oil, eggs, buttermilk and vanilla for 1 minute.

Add the dry ingredients and mix until just combined. While mixing, slowly add the hot water in a continuous stream.

Divide the batter evenly between the two prepared cake tins, then bake for 50–55 minutes, until a skewer inserted into the centre comes out clean.

Leave to cool at room temperature before placing in the freezer for a minimum of 1 hour.

Using a serrated knife, trim the tops off the chilled cakes, then slice each cake into three equal layers. Set aside.

For the chocolate ganache, combine the cream, vanilla and glucose in a saucepan over medium heat and bring to the boil.

Meanwhile, place the chocolate in a microwave-safe plastic bowl and heat in the microwave on high in 30-second increments until it is 50% melted.

Pour the hot cream mixture over the chocolate and whisk until the chocolate is completely melted and incorporated.

Cover with plastic wrap touching the surface of the ganache and leave to sit at room temperature for approximately 3 hours, until it is firm but still spreadable.

Continued overleaf >

FOR BEST RESULTS

> To create even layers, make marks around the cake where you will cut it, and cut while turning the cake until you reach the centre.

> Once you have cut the cake into layers, return them to the freezer to make handling and assembling easier.

> Use one of the cake bases, base facing upwards, as the top layer of the cake. This will ensure a flat surface on top.

> Don't let the ganache become too firm before layering the cake.

NEXT LEVEL

> You can dust the chocolate curls with edible gold lustre dust.

For the chocolate soak, combine the water, sugar and vanilla in a saucepan over high heat and bring to the boil.

Once the sugar has completely dissolved, remove from the heat, add the cocoa powder and whisk until there are no lumps remaining. Set aside to cool completely at room temperature.

For the milk chocolate curls, temper the chocolate by placing it in a microwave-safe plastic bowl and heating it in the microwave on high in 30-second increments, stirring in between. Once you have 50% solids and 50% liquid, stir vigorously until the solids have completely melted. If you have some resistant buttons, gently heat the chocolate with a hair dryer, while stirring, until melted.

Spread a small amount of the tempered chocolate in a thin layer over a stone or smooth cold work surface. Work the chocolate backwards and forwards with an offset palette knife just until it begins to go dull.

Using a metal scraper, or the blade of a knife, scrape the chocolate to create different-shaped curls.

Leave to set at room temperature.

To assemble, place the first layer of chocolate cake on a serving plate. Using a pastry brush, brush the surface of the cake generously with the chocolate soak.

Spread one-sixth of the ganache over the cake, pushing it towards the edges.

Repeat with the remaining chocolate cake layers, chocolate soak and ganache.

Top the finished cake with the chocolate curls.

The cake can be stored in the fridge for up to 5 days. Leave it to come back to room temperature before serving.

To make your own buttermilk, combine 120 ml (4 fl oz) of full-cream milk with 1 teaspoon of fresh lemon juice and leave to stand for 5 minutes before using.

Swiss Roll with White Chocolate Ganache & Strawberries

WHITE CHOCOLATE GANACHE

665 ml (22¾ fl oz) thickened (whipping) cream

1 teaspoon vanilla bean paste

25 g (1 oz) liquid glucose

190 g (6¾ oz) good-quality white chocolate

CHOCOLATE SPONGE

vegetable oil spray, for greasing

90 g (3¼ oz) caster (superfine) sugar, plus extra for sprinkling

200 g (7 oz) whole eggs, at room temperature

55 g (2 oz) plain (all-purpose) flour

30 g (1 oz) Dutch-process cocoa powder

TO ASSEMBLE

250 g (9 oz) strawberries, cut into thin wedges

pure icing (confectioners') sugar, for dusting

A timeless celebration of simplicity, this is a classic for a reason. This dreamy Swiss roll weaves together creamy white chocolate ganache and soft chocolate sponge with pops of strawberry for a luscious dessert. The sponge is perfectly light and airy, complementing the full-bodied, velvety ganache. Nostalgic, memorable and satisfying.

To make the white chocolate ganache, combine 270 ml (9½ fl oz) of the cream, the vanilla and liquid glucose in a saucepan over medium heat and bring to the boil.

Place the white chocolate in a bowl, then pour the hot cream mixture over the chocolate and whisk to combine. Add the remaining cream and whisk to incorporate.

Cover with plastic wrap touching the surface of the ganache and place in the fridge for a minimum of 6 hours.

For the chocolate sponge, preheat the oven to 190°C (375°F) fan-forced. Spray a 24 x 37 cm (9½ x 14½ inch) baking tray with sides with vegetable oil. Line the base and sides with baking paper.

In the bowl of a stand mixer with a whisk attachment, whisk the sugar and eggs on high speed for approximately 5 minutes, until light and fluffy.

Meanwhile, sift the flour and cocoa powder onto a sheet of baking paper.

To check whether the egg mixture is ready, lift the whisk and drizzle the mixture back onto itself. If it sits on top without immediately sinking back into the rest of the mixture, it is ready.

Remove the bowl from the mixer and gradually add the sifted ingredients, gently folding them through after each addition.

Pour the sponge batter into the prepared baking tray and gently spread the mixture out evenly, taking care not to knock out too much air.

Bake for 8–10 minutes, until the sponge bounces back when gently pressed.

Continued overleaf >

FIX IT

> If the sponge cracks, you can still use it and, rather than just topping the Swiss roll with whipped ganache, cover the whole roll.

> If you overwhip the ganache, add some chilled cream and gently fold it through to bring it back. If it's gone too far and the cold cream doesn't help, cover the gap between the bowl and the mixer with plastic wrap (or use the mixer's bowl shield) and whisk until you make butter. This will be delicious on toast or pancakes.

NEXT LEVEL

> Intersperse the strawberries on top with chocolate curls from my Decadent six-layer chocolate cake (see page 199).

Take a sheet of baking paper larger than your sponge, lay it flat on your work surface and sprinkle it with caster sugar.

While the sponge is still hot, turn it out onto the sugar-coated baking paper. Gently remove the baking paper that came out of the tin from the base of the sponge.

Fold the end of the sugar-covered baking paper over the short edge of the sponge and roll the paper and sponge together into a tight roll. Set aside to cool at room temperature.

Transfer the white chocolate ganache to the bowl of a stand mixer with a whisk attachment and whip on medium speed until it reaches piping consistency.

Gently unroll the chocolate sponge.

Spread three-quarters of the whipped white chocolate ganache evenly over the sponge, starting from the curled end of the sponge and leaving a 1 cm (½ inch) border at the other end.

Place the remaining whipped white chocolate ganache in the fridge until required.

Arrange two-thirds of the cut strawberries over the ganache layer, ensuring they are evenly distributed.

Starting from the curled edge, use the baking paper to lift the sponge as you roll it as tightly as possible, not including the baking paper this time.

Place a ruler on top of the baking paper where the two ends of the roll meet. Angle the ruler towards the bottom of the roulade, then push the ruler inwards while pulling on the bottom piece of baking paper to tighten the roll.

Place the roll in the fridge for 30 minutes before using a hot serrated knife to trim the ends.

Transfer the Swiss roll to a serving plate.

Using a warm teaspoon, place a line of the whipped ganache along the top of the Swiss roll.

Arrange the remaining strawberry pieces on top of the whipped ganache.

Dust with icing sugar before serving.

The sponge is best rolled when fresh. Store the completed Swiss roll in the fridge for up to 4 days.

Chocolate-dipped Orange Shortbread Fingers

SHORTBREAD

145 g (5 oz) unsalted butter

finely grated zest of 4 large oranges

130 g (4½ oz) caster (superfine) sugar

¼ teaspoon salt

65 g (2¼ oz) egg yolks

200 g (7 oz) plain (all purpose) flour

20 g (¾ oz) baking powder

CHOCOLATE DIP

1 kg (2 lb 4 oz) good-quality milk chocolate

You can't go wrong with a good shortbread, but it can be made even better by dipping it in chocolate. On the inside is rich, buttery shortbread with delectable orange notes, and on the outside is a silky chocolate coating.

To make the shortbread, grease and line a 22 cm (8½ inch) square cake tin.

In a stand mixer with a paddle attachment, mix the butter, orange zest, sugar and salt on medium speed until there are no lumps remaining.

Add the egg yolks and mix to incorporate. Lastly, add the flour and baking powder and mix until the ingredients just come together as a dough. Press the dough evenly into the prepared tin and place in the fridge for a minimum of 1 hour.

Preheat the oven to 170°C (325°F) fan-forced.

Bake the shortbread for 18–20 minutes. As soon as you remove it from the oven, gently press the raised edges around the sides with a small palette knife to level out the surface. Cool at room temperature. Once cooled, remove from the tin and cut into three even rectangles, then cut into 3 cm (1¼ inch) fingers.

For the chocolate dip, temper the chocolate by placing it in a microwave-safe plastic bowl and heating it in the microwave on high in 30-second increments, stirring in between. Once you have 50% solids and 50% liquid, stir vigorously until the solids have completely melted. If you have some resistant buttons, gently heat the chocolate with a hair dryer, while stirring, until melted.

Using a fork, dip one shortbread finger at a time in the chocolate before transferring it to a baking tray lined with baking paper. Immediately dab the surface of the chocolate with a small piece of scrunched-up plastic wrap or a clean sponge to create a rough texture. Re-melt the chocolate as necessary and repeat with the remaining shortbread fingers. Leave to set at room temperature.

These are best stored at room temperature below 25°C (77°F) in an airtight container for up to 2 weeks.

NEXT LEVEL

> Create a sleek gold finish by brushing gold lustre dust over the chocolate coating once it has set.

> You can replace the orange with other flavours, such as vanilla, cinnamon or a touch of nutmeg.

Chocolate Babka Knot with Peanut Swirl

CHOCOLATE PEANUT FILLING

70 g (2½ oz) unsalted butter

65 g (2¼ oz) caster (superfine) sugar

20 g (¾ oz) Dutch-process cocoa powder

50 g (1¾ oz) good-quality dark chocolate

75 g (2½ oz) crunchy peanut butter

BRIOCHE DOUGH

75 ml (2¼ fl oz) full-cream milk

30 g (1 oz) caster (superfine) sugar, plus 1 teaspoon

8 g (¼ oz) instant yeast

290 g (10¼ oz) plain (all-purpose) flour

100 g (3½ oz) whole eggs

1 teaspoon vanilla bean paste

pinch of salt

50 g (1¾ oz) unsalted butter, melted and cooled

vegetable oil spray

SYRUP

50 ml (1½ fl oz) water

65 g (2¼ oz) caster (superfine) sugar

Lose yourself in a maze of sweet, braided bread and explore the flavours and textures within. I love the wonderfully entwined shape of this glossy brioche. It's great for tearing and sharing, and that hint of peanut and swirl of semi-sweet chocolate takes it to a whole new level.

To make the chocolate peanut filling, melt the butter in a saucepan over medium heat. Add the sugar and whisk until dissolved. Add the cocoa powder, dark chocolate and peanut butter and whisk until completely incorporated.

Remove from the heat and transfer to a bowl. Cover with plastic wrap touching the surface.

Set aside to cool at room temperature until the mixture reaches a spreadable consistency.

For the brioche dough, warm the milk and the 1 teaspoon of caster sugar in the microwave or a saucepan until it reaches body temperature.

Add the yeast and whisk to combine. (It is important that the milk is not too hot or it will kill the yeast.) Set aside at room temperature for 5–10 minutes until it begins to froth.

In the bowl of a stand mixer with a dough hook attachment, combine the 30 g (1 oz) of caster sugar, the flour, eggs, vanilla and salt.

Add the melted and cooled butter followed by the milk and yeast mixture. Mix on low speed for 3 minutes, until the dough comes together.

Increase the mixer speed to medium and continue to mix for 8–10 minutes, until the dough begins to pull away from the side of the bowl and looks shiny.

Transfer the dough to your work surface, fold the edges into the centre and flip the dough over so that the seams are underneath. Roll the dough to create a smooth ball and transfer into a lightly greased bowl.

FOR BEST RESULTS

> To make this recipe nut free, replace the peanut butter with 30 ml (1 fl oz) of a mild oil.

FIX IT

> If the babka is colouring too quickly at the start, turn the oven down 10–15°C (50–60°F) or cover the top with foil.

> If the dough is too soft, don't try to plait it. Instead, place it in the fridge or freezer until it firms up before plaiting.

Cover the bowl with plastic wrap and leave to sit at room temperature for 1½–2 hours, until the dough has doubled in size.

Punch down the dough, then divide it into two equal portions and transfer them to separate lightly greased bowls. Cover each with plastic wrap and place in the fridge for 30 minutes.

Preheat the oven to 160°C (315°F) fan-forced. Prepare a 23 cm (9 inch) round springform tin by lining the base with baking paper and greasing the side.

Lightly oil a work surface and roll each portion of dough into a square, approximately 28 cm (11¼ inches).

Leaving a 3 mm (⅛ inch) border, spread the prepared chocolate peanut filling evenly over the two squares of dough.

Roll each square of dough into a log. With your hands, roll the logs while slowly stretching them until they are approximately 40 cm (16 inches) long. Cut each log in half lengthways. If the dough becomes soft during the rolling process, return it to the fridge to firm up.

Intertwine the four strips of dough into a basket-weave formation, ensuring the cut sides are facing up. Refer to the photos on page 212 and work your way around the formation to braid the babka.

Fold the ends of the strips underneath and transfer the braided dough to the prepared tin.

Cover the tin with plastic wrap and allow the dough to rise at room temperature for 1½ hours.

Remove the plastic wrap and transfer the dough to the oven. Bake for 30–35 minutes.

Prepare the syrup while the babka is in the oven.

In a saucepan over medium heat, boil the water and sugar until the sugar has completely dissolved.

Once baked, remove the babka from the tin. Brush the top with the syrup and serve warm.

Store at room temperature. The babka is best eaten within 4 days.

Pictured overleaf >

Acknowledgements

I am extremely grateful to have worked on this project with such a talented and passionate team. Without each and every one of you, a book like this would not be possible.

Beginning with my husband, Michael, and son, Charlie. You have simultaneously eaten and provided feedback for every recipe in this book. So much so, I believe Charlie must be made of chocolate by now. I will forever be grateful to both of you for your unwavering support, and acceptance of the endless hours I pour into my work.

A very special thank you to the team at Murdoch Books. I truly appreciate your unrelenting support and guidance throughout the entire process. To Jane Morrow for embracing my vision and making it a reality, Ariana Klepac for your attention to detail and passion for this project, Megan Pigott for your design genius and chocolate-loving ways, Trisha Garner for the design, and Justine Harding for managing the editorial.

Thank you to Joanne McLeod for your brilliance in creative writing and meticulous recipe editing. To Elle Bullen for generously sharing your talent for words – your help with this book has been monumental. Alex Williams, thank you for your organisational skills, which ensured I squeezed every last minute out of each day. Jean Kirkland, Hieu Hofor and Christean Ng, I can't thank you enough for your relentless hard work and kitchen wizardry.

Thanks to Armelle Habib for the absolutely stunning photography, and Lee Blaylock for the always-on-point styling. Not only am I grateful for your exceptional skills, but it was also a pleasure to work with two dynamic women.

A special thank you to the Savour team. Andrew Agpawa and Zac Cause for the highlights captured during this project. To Ana Trupkovic, Chantelle Al Assad and Rose Marino, your assistance has been very much appreciated.

A chocolate queen would be nowhere without her chocolate dealers. Gary Willis and Robbie Mayers from Mayers, thank you for your continual support.

A special mention to Callebaut chocolate, Bulla Family Dairy, UNOX Ovens, Tomkin and Heilala Vanilla. I'm so grateful for your ongoing support and truly value our collaborations. To Gary Isherwood, Ty Pryor and the wonderful Stone Ambassador team, thank you for your stunning backdrops and beautiful stone.

My deepest appreciation to my fans and customers – thank you for your unyielding loyalty. I have enjoyed your company throughout my chocolate journey. It's your curiosity that drives me, and my hope is to continue to inspire you on your own delicious chocolate journey.

Index

Published in 2023 by Murdoch Books,
an imprint of Allen & Unwin

Murdoch Books Australia
Cammeraygal Country
83 Alexander Street
Crows Nest NSW 2065
Phone: +61 (0)2 8425 0100
murdochbooks.com.au
info@murdochbooks.com.au

Murdoch Books UK
Ormond House
26–27 Boswell Street
London WC1N 3JZ
Phone: +44 (0) 20 8785 5995
murdochbooks.co.uk
info@murdochbooks.co.uk

For corporate orders and custom publishing,
contact our business development team
at salesenquiries@murdochbooks.com.au

Publisher: Jane Morrow
Editorial manager: Justine Harding
Design manager: Megan Pigott
Designer: Trisha Garner
Editor: Ariana Klepac
Photographer: Armelle Habib
Stylist: Lee Blaylock
Production director: Lou Playfair

*Murdoch Books acknowledges the Traditional
Owners of the Country on which we live and
work. We pay our respects to all Aboriginal and
Torres Strait Islander Elders, past and present.*

ISBN 978 1 92261 688 3

 A catalogue record for this
book is available from the
National Library of Australia

Colour reproduction by Splitting Image
Colour Studio Pty Ltd, Wantirna, Victoria
Printed by C&C Offset Printing Co. Ltd., China

OVEN GUIDE: All oven temperatures listed
are fan-forced unless otherwise stated. If you
require the conventional oven temperature,
increase the given temperature by 15–20°C
(25–35°F), according to the manufacturer's
instructions.

TABLESPOON MEASURES: We have used
20 ml (4 teaspoon) tablespoon measures.
If you are using a 15 ml (3 teaspoon) tablespoon
add an extra teaspoon of the ingredient for
each tablespoon specified.

10   9   8   7   6   5   4   3   2   1